H-RABBITPIE

ti to: 7 CHEESE

steak and kidney pie

It is so difficult to give a recipe for this most famous of pies as opinions on the definitive version vary widely. However, the theme they all seem to share is a long, slow cooking time for the meat, to give a rich, dark stew with a glossy gravy. They also all agree that the filling tastes best when made up to two days ahead and that a deep earthenware dish should be used for the pie and a good puff or flaky pastry for the lid. My butcher reckons that the best cut of meat for slow cooking is chuck steak, which creates a wonderful gravy, and that pigs' kidneys provide the best flavour.

serves 6

for the pastry
400g/13oz flaky pastry (see page 19) · beaten egg, to glaze

for the filling
25g/1oz plain flour · 900g/1³/₄lb chuck steak, cut into 2.5cm/1in cubes · 225g/8oz pigs' kidneys, cut into 2.5cm/1in cubes · 25g/1oz butter · 2 large onions, finely sliced · 1 tbsp chopped fresh thyme · 150g/5oz chestnut mushrooms, roughly chopped · 300ml/¹/₂ pint red wine 300ml/¹/₂ pint beef stock · 2 tbsp Worcestershire sauce · salt and ground black pepper

Preheat the oven to 180°C/350°F/Gas 4.

Place the flour in a large mixing bowl and add the steak and kidneys. Season with a little salt and plenty of ground black pepper. Toss well until the meat is completely coated with flour.

Heat the butter in a large, heavy-based casserole dish and cook the onions until just softened but not browned. Add the meat, thyme and mushrooms and brown the meat quickly on all sides. Add any leftover flour and pour in the wine, stock and Worcestershire sauce. Bring to the boil, cover and place in the oven for 1¹/₂ hours until the meat is tender and the gravy thick and glossy. Transfer the meat and gravy into a 2 litre/3¹/₂ pint deep pie dish and leave to cool.

Increase the oven temperature to 200°C/400°F/Gas 6.

Roll out the pastry to a thickness of about 3mm/¹/₈in. Cut a 2cm/³/₄in strip from the rolled-out pastry. Brush the rim of the pie dish with water and place the pastry strip around the rim, pressing

for my mum and dad and craig, without whom this book would never have happened

Art direction and design Vanessa Courtier · **Food styling** Angela Boggiano · **Publishing manager** Anna Cheifetz

Angela's Assistant Jules Mercer · **Recipe still-life photography** Craig Robertson · **Location and reportage photography** Vanessa Courtier

First published in Great Britain in 2006 by Cassell Illustrated,
a division of Octopus Publishing Group Limited
2–4 Heron Quays, London E14 4JP

Reprinted 2007

Text copyright © Angela Boggiano   Design and layout © Cassell Illustrated

The moral right of Angela Boggiano to be identified as the author of this Work has been asserted
in accordance with the Copyright, Designs and Patents Act of 1988

Distributed in the United States of America by Sterling Publishing Co., Inc., 387 Park Avenue South, New York, NY 10016-8810

A CIP catalogue record for this book is available from the British Library.

ISBN-13: 978-1-844034-48-2
ISBN-10: 1-844034-48-8
10 9 8 7 6 5 4 3 2 1

Printed in China

pie

Angela Boggiano

photography by Vanessa Courtier and Craig Robertson

contents

"

I've always loved pies. Making them, eating them, watching how other people make them, talking about them. In fact, talking about them was probably what inspired me to write this book more than anything else. I began to realise what an emotional issue pies are for many people. Almost everyone has a favourite pie, and with that pie comes a story, often about a family member or childhood memory. Favourite pies are not necessarily gourmet pies – usually a humble apple pie that Auntie Maureen used to make or a pork pie from the local butchers. It's often the nostalgia and comforting thoughts they conjure up that make the pies seem to taste all the more delicious.

As I carried out more and more research, I realised just how large a part pie making plays in this country's heritage. Britain is steeped in pie-making traditions, from Cornish pasties to game pies. It's easy to see why pies are so popular; a pie is a warming, filling complete meal in itself – eaten in the hand for lunches and picnics as well as a hearty main meal. Actually, I think the pie is the greatest invention ever, but maybe that makes me a bit of a pie obsessive!

As well as tasty recipes, I wanted to include stories of pie makers old and new from the wonderful heritage of the famous pie and mash shops to the modern pie café with its contemporary fillings. That's why this book contains a collection of traditional recipes, such as stargazy pie and raised pies with hot-water crust pastry, alongside more modern pies with tasty fillings, like lamb, pumpkin and mint or curried football pie.

Pies don't need fancy fillings with hundreds of ingredients – they can be relatively simple – but the ingredients do need to be of high quality to make a pie really stand out. If you always choose good meat you won't need to do much to the filling apart from cooking it slowly to capture its delicious flavour. Tasty local and regional cheeses, seasonal fruits and vegetables can only add to a successful end result.

Making a spectacular pie will give you a real sense of achievement. Perhaps it's because pie making does take a bit of time and effort that the sense of satisfaction is so great. But – and this is the big but – despite the effort, pie making is not something to be scared of, and I hope that's what you'll find with this collection of recipes. I wanted to take away the fear of pastry making – which is what stops most people making pies – because the fillings are generally straightforward. I want everybody to make pies and to create a new generation of pie makers so that all the fascinating history surrounding them is not lost. Go forth and bake!

historypies

Since recipes have first been recorded, the pie has held an honoured place in the history of cooking. Certainly the British have as great a claim as any nation to being the ultimate exponents of the art of pie making. From the earliest medieval recipes to substantial eighteenth-century pies, a tradition has grown up that is an integral part of our culinary heritage.

There is evidence, however, that the ancient Egyptians may have been the first to indulge, and that recipes were passed from Egypt to classical Greece and then to Rome and the rest of Europe. In the earliest recipes it is clear that the pastry was never eaten but used merely as a container to be thrown away and as a malleable material to make sculptural forms. Known as 'subtleties', these forms became very popular in medieval England and were used as centrepieces for banqueting tables. The English were also responsible for creating pastry using suet and fat (later butter), in place of the oil used by the Romans. This allowed the evolution of finer and more delicate pastry, which ultimately could be eaten.

The great advantage of the pie has always been that it allows for a range of ingredients to be cooked together in a pastry crust, making it as popular in the banqueting hall as in the home. The only differentiation has been in the ingredients used. Traditionally, the lowest form of pie was 'umble pie', made from the entrails of deer and served to the less fortunate diners at the medieval dinner table (where the phrase 'to eat humble pie' was coined). More esteemed diners might, however, be tucking into a delicious venison pie, or perhaps a pie of seasonal fruits.

Pies were versatile, portable and easy to cook; and the discovery that pouring clarified butter into the pastry casing excluded any air and preserved the contents for a time only increased pies' popularity, as they could be stored and transported further afield – the ultimate travelling fare.

With recipes taken to America and Australia by the first English settlers, the pie furthered its global domination. From savoury to sweet, shortcrust to flaky, today's favourite pies are now the culmination of a long and varied heritage that continues to inform every exciting new filling and delicious pie creation.

basicpie

For me, the best bit of a pie is the golden pastry, so the more there is of that the better. Making pastry isn't difficult if you follow a few simple rules and master the basic techniques – there's a lot of truth in the old saying 'as easy as pie'. Home-made pastry always has a better flavour than shop-bought and it's this taste and texture which make the process really worthwhile and quite satisfying. One of the benchmarks of cooking, however, is authenticity, and mastering the classic look of the 'turned-out' pie-shop pie can become a labour of love. Producing a beautiful home-made pie involves a number of stages and it can't be simply bashed out. So, whether you opt for making your own or using shop-bought, pastry will always require a little patience and respect.

Here are my golden rules for achieving perfect results when making your own pastry:

1 Handle it lightly
2 Keep it cool
3 Bake it in a hot oven

all you need for pastry

Hands   Cool hands are the cook's most valuable asset.

Flour   Plain white all-purpose flour is the most widely used flour for shortcrust pastry. Self-raising flour produces a much softer pastry, which can be a little difficult to handle, and gives a very crumbly texture when you want a crisp pastry.

Choose a strong plain flour for flaky, rough and puff pastry and a breadmaking flour for hot-water crust pastry (as for this you need plenty of gluten to shape the pastry). The best way to store flour is in its own bag (as this will have the use-by date on it) in a cool dry place. Try not to mix new flour with old stock.

Fat   The fat is such an important feature in pastry, as it determines the texture as well as the taste. Always weigh your fat carefully – too much fat will make the pastry unmanageable and very short (crumbly) and too little will make it hard. Lard is the vital ingredient in hot-water crust pastry.

A mixture of lard and butter makes a very good shortcrust pastry as the lard gives it a short, light and crisp texture and the butter imparts a delicious flavour. Don't be tempted to substitute margarine as it contains water and will result in a tough crust. Ensure that the fat is cool but not straight from the fridge as this makes it tricky to handle.

Eggs   Egg yolks are added to pastry to enrich the dough, creating a rich shortcrust pastry. Eggs are also used for glazes, especially on savoury pies. A mixture of equal quantities of egg yolk and water and a pinch of salt gives the best ever golden glaze.

Liquid   Water is the main liquid used in pastry making, but milk can also be added. Adding soured cream or yoghurt will make a tender pastry, ideal for en croûtes and wrapping pâtés. Pastry with a high fat content and the addition of egg yolks needs hardly any water. In most cases the liquid should be chilled so that it does not soften or melt the fat. The exception is hot-water crust pastry where the fat and liquid must be hot. Be careful when adding the liquid – too much will make your pastry sticky and difficult to handle and tough when cooked; too little and it will be dry and may crack.

Containers   For the best results when making a double-crust pie, use a metallic pie dish. I use enamel dishes, which work well as they come in various sizes and are inexpensive. Ceramic dishes just don't conduct the heat well enough to get the bottom of the pie crisp.

Pie plates have a wide rim and are usually made of metal. They are quite shallow and can also be used to make a double-crust pie, which can then be cut into wedges for serving.

Deep earthenware pie dishes, which can be round or oval, are great for rich, robust, savoury or sweet fillings that are quite chunky and require only one crust of pastry on the top.

Raised pie moulds are ideal for raised game and meat pies. They are normally hinged on one side so that you can remove the pie easily when it is cooked. They also often have patterned sides which give the pie an embossed appearance when it is turned out.

Pie funnel   This ceramic funnel acts as a chimney as the pie filling cooks, letting out steam which might otherwise make the pastry soggy and prevent it from rising properly. The funnel also provides extra support for the pastry.

Baking tray   A heavy-duty baking tray is a real asset for crisping the pastry on the bottom of your pie. Place the baking sheet in a hot oven for about 15 minutes to heat up thoroughly, then sit the pie on the hot tray and bake. The heat from the tray will help to ensure a crispy bottom. The tray will also catch any spillages from the pie if the filling bubbles out (which certainly saves on the oven cleaning!).

Rolling pin   A rolling pin is, of course, essential for rolling out the pastry. A thick, heavy, wooden one will do the job well. When rolling, always ensure that the pastry is cold and lightly flour the rolling pin rather than the pastry. This will stop you from adding too much flour to the pastry (which will make it dry and crumbly) and will prevent the rolling pin sticking to the pastry surface. Roll out your pastry using gentle strokes to avoid overstretching it (which will make it tough). Always chill shortcrust pastry before rolling, even if only for a short time. This will allow the gluten to 'relax' and helps prevent the pastry from shrinking when it is cooked.

quantities and sizes

When a recipe calls for 300g/10oz of pastry this means that it should be made with 200g/7oz of flour. This is because the weight of the pastry also includes the weight of the fat (so pastry made with 300g/10oz of flour really weighs in at 450g/14½oz).

200g/7oz flour = 300g/10oz pastry · 300g/10oz flour = 450g/14½oz pastry
400g/13oz flour = 600g/1¼lb pastry

single-crust pie
300g/10oz pastry covers a 600ml/1 pint dish · 400g/13oz pastry covers a 1.5–2 litre/2½–3½ pint dish · 600g/1¼lb pastry covers a 2.5 litre/4 pint dish

double-crust pie
300g/10oz pastry lines and covers an 18cm/7in dish 450g/14¼oz pastry lines and covers a 23cm/9in dish · 600g/1¼lb pastry lines and covers a 30cm/12in dish

shortcrust pastry

This is a great all-purpose pastry which is robust and easy to handle. The proportions to remember are half fat to flour, with enough liquid to combine. I've tried other quantities but I always end up coming back to this pastry mantra and it works perfectly every time.

This is the simplest and most widely used pastry and is suitable for either sweet or savoury pies. The mixture of butter and lard or white vegetable fat really is the best combination for flavour and texture, producing a light, crisp texture and delicious, buttery taste. If you don't want to use lard simply substitute a white vegetable fat – you will find a whole selection to choose from and they are all pretty much the same. When making a sweet pie, add 2 tablespoons of caster sugar to the mix.

makes 300g/10oz of pastry
200g/7oz plain flour · pinch salt · 50g/2oz butter · 50g/2oz lard or white vegetable fat
2–3 tbsp water, to mix

Mix the flour and salt in a bowl. Cut the fat into cubes and add this to the flour. Use your fingertips to rub the fat into the flour until the mixture resembles fine breadcrumbs. Add the water very gradually, stirring it in with a knife. When the dough just sticks together, knead it lightly until it forms a ball. Wrap in cling film and allow to rest for at least 15 minutes in the fridge. It can be left in the fridge for up to 2 days. Alternatively it can be frozen until ready to use.

Once you have the basic mixture you can flavour it with toasted ground spices, chopped fresh herbs or toasted and finely chopped nuts.

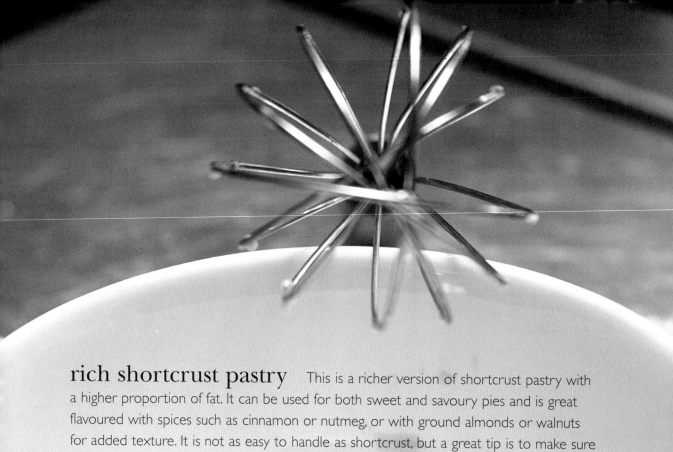

rich shortcrust pastry
This is a richer version of shortcrust pastry with a higher proportion of fat. It can be used for both sweet and savoury pies and is great flavoured with spices such as cinnamon or nutmeg, or with ground almonds or walnuts for added texture. It is not as easy to handle as shortcrust, but a great tip is to make sure it is perfectly chilled, then roll out between two sheets of greaseproof paper. This prevents it from sticking to the worksurface or rolling pin and makes it easy to transfer to the pie dish. Adding lemon juice stops the gluten in the flour from developing and will prevent the pastry from being too tough. Lemon juice can be added to any of the short pastry recipes. When making a sweet pie, add 2 tablespoons of icing sugar for sweetness.

makes 300g/10oz of pastry
200g/7oz plain flour · ¹/₄ tsp salt · 2 tbsp icing sugar, if making sweet pastry · 100g/3¹/₂oz unsalted butter, cold · I egg, beaten · I tsp lemon juice · 2 tbsp iced water

Mix together the flour and salt (and icing sugar, if making a sweet pastry). Chop the butter into cubes and add half of it to the flour. Gently and swiftly rub the fat into the flour until it resembles coarse breadcrumbs. Add the rest of the butter and mix until it's the size of small peas. Make a well in the centre of the dry ingredients. Mix the beaten egg with the lemon juice and water and gradually pour into the well a little at a time, using a knife to mix the dough as you go. If the mixture looks like it has sufficient liquid to form a dough, don't add all the liquid as the absorbency of flours varies. Turn out on to a floured board and knead lightly until smooth. Shape into a ball, wrap in cling film and refrigerate for at least 30 minutes before use.

cheese pastry
This is great for enriching savoury pies but also works beautifully for sweet fruit pies too, such as the Apple Pie on page 164. You can experiment with different cheeses for this pastry, but ones with a strong flavour such as Red Leicester, Parmesan, mature Cheddar and Gruyère work best. Add a pinch of mustard powder for extra oomph.

makes 400g/13oz of pastry
200g/7oz plain flour · pinch salt · 150g/5oz butter · 50g/2oz hard cheese, such as mature Cheddar or Parmesan, grated · 2–3 tbsp water, to mix

Mix the flour and salt in a bowl. Cut the fat into pieces and add this to the flour. Use your fingertips to rub the fat into the flour until the mixture resembles fine breadcrumbs. Stir in the cheese, then add the water very gradually, stirring it in with a knife. When the dough just sticks together, knead it lightly into a ball, wrap in cling film and allow it to rest for at least 15 minutes in the fridge.

flaky and puff pastries

It's quite tricky and time-consuming to make these rich flaky pastries, which is why most people resort to the simpler alternative of buying ready-made. These are now of a very high standard, so I've given recipes only for the simpler types of flaky and rough puff pastry. The very high fat content of puff pastry is what makes it rich and fine, but can also cause it to be difficult to handle. As with all pastries, though, a little practice will make perfect.

It is the rolling and folding procedure that ensures the fat and flour remain in layers, giving a crisp flaky pastry.

flaky pastry

This is a wonderful pastry to make if you're pulling out all the stops. If you've spent a lot of time, effort and perhaps money creating a fantastic filling for a pie, then it only makes sense to finish it off with a wonderful topping. Obviously this is not one for everyday pies. When baked, the pastry looks a little like puff pastry but has fewer layers. The fat is incorporated by dotting it over the rolled-out dough. This creates pockets of air and helps to separate the layers.

makes 400g/13oz of pastry
200g/7oz plain flour · 1/4 tsp salt · 75g/3oz butter, softened · 75g/3oz lard or vegetable fat, softened
150ml/1/4 pint water · 1 tsp lemon juice

First sift the flour with the salt. In a large bowl mix together the softened butter and lard or vegetable fat and divide into four equal portions. Rub one of these portions into the flour and mix to a soft dough with the water and lemon juice.

Roll this pastry into an oblong three times as long as it is wide measuring 30 x 10cm/12 x 4in. Dot another quarter of the fat over the top two-thirds of the rolled-out pastry. Fold the bottom third up and the top third down. Turn the dough sideways. Press down the edges of the pastry to seal the fat inside. Roll out again and repeat this procedure until all the fat is used up. Leave the pastry to rest for 5 minutes between each turn. Wrap in cling film and leave to chill in the fridge for at least 30 minutes.

When ready to use, roll out to 3mm/1/4in thick. Should the pastry become warm and sticky at any time, wrap it in cling film and chill for about 15 minutes before continuing.

short cut flaky pastry

This is so easy to make and gives really great results – you just have to be a bit organised and get the butter in the freezer in advance. In this version, instead of dotting the dough with the fat, you can grate or shred it into the flour. The resulting pastry has the same buttery flavour and crispness as flaky pastry but is not as light.

makes 450g/14 1/4oz of pastry
200g/7oz butter · 350g/11 1/2oz plain flour · pinch salt · 6 tbsp chilled water

Place the butter in the freezer for about 20 minutes until it is very hard. Sift the flour and salt into a mixing bowl. Hold the butter using a piece of parchment paper or greaseproof paper and grate it into the flour, working quickly. Stir the butter and flour together, sprinkle with water, and mix to make a dough, adding a little more water if needed. Wrap in cling film and chill for about 30 minutes before using.

rough puff pastry

Compared to flaky and puff pastry, this is much more straightforward and I would recommend it for rich pies such as game and venison. The end result is well worth it and incredibly satisfying.

makes about 400g/13oz of pastry
200g/7oz plain flour · 1/4 tsp salt · 75g/3oz butter · 75g/3oz lard or white vegetable fat
100ml/3 1/2fl oz cold water · 1 tsp lemon juice

Mix together the flour and salt. Cut both the fats into small cubes (this is where it differs from flaky pastry). Mix the fat into the flour without breaking up the lumps. Mix to a stiff dough with the water and lemon juice.

On a floured board, roll the dough into a strip three times as long as it is wide – about 30 x 10cm/12 x 4in. Fold the top third down and bottom third up. Turn the pastry sideways and seal the edges. Continue to roll and fold four times altogether. Leave the pastry to rest for 15 minutes between each folding and rolling. Wrap in cling film and leave to rest and chill in the fridge for 30 minutes before using.

potato pastry

This is a substantial pastry with a really crumbly texture when baked. Roll it out quite thickly and use it as a single crust on chunky meat pies.

makes 400g/13oz of pastry
100g/3 1/2oz floury potatoes, peeled and diced · 100g/3 1/2oz butter, diced · 200g/7oz plain flour
1 egg, beaten

Cook the diced potatoes in a pan of salted water until tender. Drain well and mash until smooth. Now rub the butter into the flour until the mixture resembles fine breadcrumbs. Mix together the beaten egg and a little water and stir into the mashed potato. Add to the flour mixture and stir with a round-bladed knife to form a smooth, pliable dough. Wrap in cling film and chill in the fridge for about 30 minutes before using.

wholemeal pastry

This pastry is best made with half plain and half wholemeal flour as wholemeal flour has a high proportion of coarse bran and is a little too heavy and tough when used alone for pastry. Add the water carefully, as wholemeal flour can take up a good deal of moisture and adding too much water can make the pastry very hard and crisp.

makes 300g/10oz of pastry
100g/3¹/₂oz wholemeal flour · 100g/3¹/₂oz plain flour · pinch mustard powder · pinch salt
100g/3¹/₂oz butter · 2–3 tbsp cold water, to mix

Mix together the flours, mustard powder and salt. Cut the fat into cubes and add this to the flour.
Use your fingertips to rub the fat into the flour until the mixture resembles fine breadcrumbs. Add the
water very gradually, stirring it in with a knife. When the dough just sticks together, knead it lightly into
a ball. Wrap in cling film and allow to rest for at least 15 minutes in the fridge before use.

hot-water crust
This pastry gets its name from the hot water which is added to make
a malleable dough strong enough to hold the filling. It is used for making raised pies such as pork pies,
raised game pies and Scotch pies. The addition of just a little icing sugar increases the richness of the
pastry without adding sweetness.

makes about 500g/1lb of pastry
450g/14¹/₂oz plain flour · ¹/₂ tsp salt · 1 tbsp icing sugar · 1 egg, beaten · 200ml/7fl oz water
80g/3oz butter · 80g/3oz lard

Mix the flour, salt and icing sugar in a large bowl. Make a dip in the middle, pour the egg into it and toss
a liberal covering of flour over the egg. Put the water, butter and lard into a saucepan and bring slowly to
the boil. Once the liquid is boiling, pour it on to the flour, mixing with a knife as you go. Knead until all the
egg streaks have gone and the pastry is smooth. Use immediately to make your pie as when the pastry
cools it will harden and will then be unmanageable.

wheat-free pastry

This is a recipe that I have used again and again and in my experience works really well. The problem with a wheat-free pastry is trying to achieve the same stretchy consistency you get with wheat pastry. It is the gluten in wheat flour which gives the pastry its texture. A solution to this is to add xanthan gum, which is readily available in health-food shops. This is a white powder which, when mixed with non-wheat flours and liquid, makes the pastry stretchy and easy to roll out. Gluten-free flour (such as Doves Farm) is also now available in major supermarkets. It can make the dough crumbly and difficult to roll, but with patience it will prove a great substitute.

makes 300g/10oz of pastry
75g/3oz rice flour · 75g/3oz fine cornmeal (polenta) · 75g/3oz potato flour · pinch salt
150g/5oz butter, cut into cubes · I egg · 2 tbsp cold water · I tsp xanthan gum

Place the rice flour, cornmeal, potato flour and salt in a bowl and mix together well. Add the butter to the dry ingredients and carefully rub together with your fingertips until the mixture resembles breadcrumbs. Mix the egg with the water and xanthan gum and add to the flour and butter a little at a time. You might find that the mixture comes together to make a dough before you have added all the liquid; this is fine — don't be tempted to add it all, as flours have different levels of absorbency. Tip the dough out onto a lightly floured surface and knead for a few minutes until silky smooth. Wrap in cling film and refrigerate for 30 minutes until ready to use. Use as for shortcrust pastry.

food processor pastry

If you happen to have a food processor, this method for making pastry is great for speed and ease. It is particularly good for rich pastry and sweet pastry, where the higher proportions of fat and sugar can make the dough difficult to handle with warm hands. A food processor ensures that the dough stays cool.

makes 300g/10oz of pastry
200g/7oz plain flour · pinch salt · 2 tbsp caster sugar, if making sweet shortcrust · 50g/2oz butter, cut into cubes · 50g/2oz lard or white vegetable fat, cut into cubes · 2–3 tbsp water, to mix

Place the flour and salt (and sugar if making sweet shortcrust) in the food processor and blitz for 4–5 seconds. Scatter the cubes of butter and lard or vegetable fat over the dry ingredients. Process for 10 seconds only, or until the mixture resembles fine breadcrumbs. Sprinkle the water over the flour mixture and use the pulse button to process until the dough starts to hold together. It should feel neither too dry nor too wet. Remove the mixture from the processor and form it into a ball. Lightly knead on a floured surface for a few seconds until smooth, then wrap in cling film and chill for 30 minutes before using.

trouble shooting

faults in shortcrust pastry

Soggy bottom pastry   This may occur if your filling contains too much liquid. Your pie dish may also be too thick and not conduct the heat to the pastry efficiently. The oven may not be hot enough, or the pie may have been placed too high in the oven and cooked too quickly. Make sure the oven is at the right temperature and bake the pie on a preheated baking tray. The filling needs to be fridge-cold or it will begin to steam the pastry and make it go soggy before you bake it.

Pastry shrinks when cooked   Because pastry is tense after being rolled out, it needs to relax in the fridge for at least 30 minutes before cooking. Placing the dough in the freezer, to take it from relaxed to super-chilled, can prevent shrinkage. Be gentle when rolling out and don't overstretch the pastry.

Pastry is crumbly and hard to handle   Adding too much fat and overmixing or adding too little liquid can make pastry crumbly. It is vital to weigh ingredients carefully and handle the dough gently.

Cooked pastry is tough   This occurs when too little fat and too much liquid are added. Be careful not to overhandle the dough and make sure the oven is hot.

faults in flaky and puff pastries

Pastry hard and tough   Too much water has been added to the flour but not enough fat. It is important to keep the pastry cool during rolling and the oven needs to be hot.

Pastry not risen   The fat may have been too warm and has blended with the flour instead of remaining in layers. Make sure you rest the pastry sufficiently between rollings.

Pastry soggy in the middle   This is a result of the pastry being undercooked. Don't place the pastry on too high a shelf in the oven.

faults in hot-water crust pastry

Pastry won't mould   The fat and water may have been too cold when added to the flour, or you have used insufficient fat and water.

Crust bursts during cooking   The crust may have been unevenly moulded, making some parts thinner than others.

Crust collapses when removed from mould   The pastry could be too warm and too thin. Ensure that the pastry is chilled before removing it from the mould before baking.

homepie

Comforting, tasty and satisfying, home pies made with love are the perfect solution to a cold wintry day, feeding a hungry family, or making a special treat for friends.

No one could resist a deep, single-crusted, juicy and tender meat pie served in an earthenware dish and topped with light flaky or puff pastry. Or a simple double-crusted pie baked in a pie tin or plate which you can cut and come back to again and again. These are the pies we love to eat with family and friends and investing just a little time and attention will allow you to produce something that will impress every time.

If you use good-quality ingredients and leave enough time for slow cooking, everything else will be pretty straightforward. Sit back and enjoy everyone's delight as the decisive moment arrives and you cut into the pie, releasing an archetypal puff of steam and the divine aroma.

This recipe came from my friend David Herbert, who developed it after overcooking lamb shanks and rescuing them by putting them into a pie.

braised lamb shank pie

The lamb in this pie cooks down until it is incredibly tender, falling apart to make a tasty and succulent filling. It deserves to be topped by a rich, rough puff pastry lid.

serves 6

for the pastry
400g/13oz rough puff pastry (see page 20)
beaten egg, to glaze

for the filling
50g/2oz plain flour · 6 lamb shanks · 2 tbsp olive oil · 4 red onions, quartered · 8 cloves garlic, peeled · 1 bottle full-bodied red wine · 300ml/1/2 pint beef stock · 2 tbsp finely chopped rosemary · 3 tbsp redcurrant jelly · salt and ground black pepper

Season the flour with a good pinch of salt and plenty of ground black pepper. Dust the shanks in the seasoned flour. Heat the oil in a large saucepan or heavy-based casserole dish and brown the shanks all over. Add any remaining flour, the onions and garlic and stir well. Pour in the wine, stock, rosemary, redcurrant jelly and a good grinding of black pepper.

Bring to the boil, cover, and turn down the heat to cook at a very gentle simmer for about 2 hours until the meat falls off the bone and the sauce is rich and thickened. Remove the bones from the pan, reserving three of them, and flake the meat into small pieces.

Preheat the oven to 200°C/400°F/Gas 6.

Fill a 2 litre/3 1/2 pint pie dish with the lamb filling. Roll out the pastry to about 3mm/1/8in thick and about 2.5cm/1in larger than the dish. Cut a 2cm/3/4in strip from the pastry. Brush the rim of the dish with a little water and place the pastry strip around the rim, pressing it down. Sit the 3 reserved lamb bones in the pie filling at intervals along the length of the dish. These will act as pie funnels, releasing the steam when the pie is baking, and will also stop the pastry from sinking into the filling and becoming soggy. Cut 3 slits in the remaining pastry at the same intervals as the lamb bones.
Place the pastry lid over the top and slide it over the bones. Press down the edges of the pastry to seal. Trim off any excess pastry and crimp the edges with a fork or between your thumb and fore-finger. Brush with beaten egg and bake for 30–35 minutes until the pastry is crisp and golden.

it down. Cut out the remaining pastry about 2.5cm/1in larger than the dish. Sit a pie funnel in the centre of the filling to support the pastry and stop it from sinking into the filling and becoming soggy. Place the pastry lid over the top of the filling and press down the edges to seal. Trim off any excess pastry and crimp the edges with a fork, or between your thumb and forefinger. Brush the top of the pie with beaten egg and make a hole in the centre to reveal the pie funnel. Bake for 30–35 minutes until the pastry is crisp and golden.

steak and oyster pie   This old-fashioned recipe was a Victorian favourite.
Oysters replace kidneys to give the gravy a slight taste of the sea – it sounds a little mad but, believe me, it makes the most delicious filling for a pie. This recipe is best made as individual pies.

Buy 8 fresh rock oysters, open them and remove the flesh from the shells.
Simply prepare the Steak and Kidney Pie, as above, leaving out the kidneys. Spoon the cooled beef filling into 4 individual pie dishes. Sit 2 rock oysters on the top of each pie filling. Roll out the pastry (as above) and cut out pie lids for the individual pies. Brush the edges of the pastry with beaten egg, lay over the filling and press the edges on to the rims of the dishes. Cut a slit in the middle of each lid and brush with beaten egg. Rest in the fridge for 30 minutes then bake in a preheated oven, 200°C/400°F/Gas 6, for 30 minutes until the pastry is golden.

rabbit pot pie with polenta crust

Rabbit pies have been made in many different ways over the centuries. Generally the meat is cooked first, then placed in an earthenware pot sealed with a pastry lid to keep in the flavour. I've used this method here to create a really wonderful, tasty pie. The pastry is simply draped over the top of the dish, making it a very simple pie to prepare, but it both looks and tastes very impressive. When making the filling, bear in mind that wild rabbit has a much stronger flavour and needs a little more cooking time than the farmed variety.

serves 4

for the pastry
300g /10oz shortcrust pastry (see page 15), 50g/2oz of the flour replaced with coarse polenta beaten egg, to glaze · 4 tbsp grated Parmesan cheese

for the filling
25g/1oz butter · 1 rabbit, cut into pieces · 100g/3¹/₂oz piece pancetta, diced
1 onion, finely chopped · 2 tbsp plain flour · 300ml/¹/₂ pint white wine · 150ml/¹/₄ pint double cream · 4 cloves garlic, bruised · 2 sprigs rosemary · salt and ground black pepper

Heat the butter in a large frying pan and cook the rabbit pieces until browned (cook it in batches if necessary). Remove from the pan, add the pancetta and cook for 4 minutes until golden. Add the onion and cook for 4 minutes until the onion has softened.

Add the flour and stir for 1 minute, then add the white wine and simmer rapidly. Stir in the cream and garlic and season with a little salt and plenty of ground black pepper. Return the rabbit to the pan with a sprig of rosemary and simmer on a very low heat for 20–25 minutes until the sauce has reduced and thickened.

Preheat the oven to 200°C/400°F/Gas 6.

Spoon the mix into 1 large or 4 individual earthenware pie dishes and roll out the pastry to fit the top, allowing it to drape over the edges. Brush with beaten egg, sprinkle with Parmesan and leaves from the remaining rosemary sprig. Bake for 30 minutes.

venison pie with thyme, mustard and shallots

This wonderful pie has a rich and flavoursome filling and deserves the perfect flaky crust. The large amount of mustard gives a real depth of flavour and a wonderful creamy texture. It's certainly not an everyday dinner.

serves 6

for the pastry
450g/14¹/₂oz short-cut flaky pastry (see page 19) · beaten egg, to glaze

for the filling
40g/1¹/₂oz dried wild mushrooms · 25g/1oz plain flour · 1 tbsp fresh thyme
1kg/2lb diced venison · 2 tbsp olive oil · 400g/13oz shallots, peeled and left whole
2 cloves garlic, chopped · 2 tbsp dark muscovado sugar · 500ml/17fl oz ale, such as Theakston's
Old Peculier · 300ml/¹/₂ pint beef stock · 2 tbsp Worcestershire sauce · 2 tbsp Dijon mustard
salt and ground black pepper

Place the mushrooms in a small bowl and pour over boiling water to soak. Set aside whilst you
prepare the rest of the filling.

Place the flour in a large bowl, add the thyme and cubed venison and toss well. Season with a little
salt and a good grinding of black pepper.

Heat 1 tablespoon of the oil in a deep, flameproof casserole dish and fry the shallots for 4–5 minutes
until beginning to colour and soften. Add the garlic and toss with the shallots over a medium heat for
a minute. Remove from the dish and set aside.

Add the remaining oil to the casserole dish and brown one batch of venison on all sides, remove
and set aside. Repeat with the remaining venison. Return all the meat to the pan along with the fried
shallots and garlic. Stir in the muscovado sugar and heat through for a few minutes. Stir in the ale and
beef stock, the Worcestershire sauce, Dijon mustard, mushrooms and 100ml/3¹/₂fl oz of the soaking
liquid from the mushrooms. Season and bring gently to the boil. Cover and simmer gently for 2 hours
until the meat is tender and the sauce is glossy and thickened. Spoon into a 2 litre/3¹/₂ pint deep pie
dish and set aside to cool completely.

Preheat the oven to 200°C/400°F/Gas 6.

Roll out the pastry to a thickness of about 3mm/¹/₈in. Cut a 2cm/³/₄in strip from the rolled-out
pastry. Brush the rim of the pie dish with water and place the pastry strip around the rim, pressing
it down. Cut out a lid from the remaining pastry about 2.5cm/1in larger than the dish. Sit a pie
funnel into the centre of the filling to support the pastry and stop it from sinking into the filling and
becoming soggy. Place the pastry lid over the top and press down on the edges to seal. Trim off
any excess pastry and crimp the edges with a fork, or between your thumb and forefinger. Brush
the top with beaten egg and make a hole in the centre to reveal the pie funnel. Use the pastry
trimmings to make decorations for the top of the pie. Bake for 30–35 minutes until the pastry is
crisp and golden.

beef and ale pie

A classic rich and flavoursome home pie. The addition of ale, such as Guinness or stout, gives a real richness to the sauce. This pie is even better if you make the filling the day before, so that the stew has time to cool down and thicken up a little and the flavours can really develop. It is crying out for mashed potatoes to soak up all the delicious juices.

serves 4–6

for the pastry
300g/10oz rich shortcrust pastry (see page 16) · beaten egg, to glaze

for the filling
25g/1oz plain flour · 900g/1³/4lb chuck steak, cut into 2.5cm/1in cubes · 20g/³/4oz butter
1 tbsp vegetable oil · 2 large onions, thinly sliced · 2 carrots, chopped into 2.5cm/1in cubes
2 tsp Worcestershire sauce · 2 tsp tomato purée · 500ml/17fl oz ale such as Guinness or stout
300ml/¹/2 pint hot beef stock · 2 tsp sugar · salt and ground black pepper

Place the flour in a large bowl and season with salt and ground black pepper, add the cubes of meat and toss well in the flour until evenly coated.

Heat the butter and oil in a large, heavy-based, flameproof casserole dish until the butter has melted. Add the meat to the fat in small batches and brown quickly all over for just a minute, then remove with a slotted spoon and set aside. Add the onions and carrots to the pan and fry gently for about 2 minutes, then return the meat to the pan with the Worcestershire sauce, tomato purée, ale, stock and sugar. Grind in plenty of black pepper and add a little salt, stir well and bring to the boil. Cover, reduce to a gentle simmer and cook very slowly for 2 hours until the meat is tender and the sauce has thickened and is glossy. Remove from the heat, place into a 1.5 litre/2¹/2 pint deep pie dish and leave to cool completely.

Preheat the oven to 200°C/400°F/Gas 6.

Roll out the pastry to a thickness of about 3mm/¹/8in. Cut a 2cm/³/4in strip from the rolled-out pastry. Brush the rim of the pie dish with water and place the pastry strip around the rim, pressing it down. Cut out the remaining pastry about 2.5cm/1in larger than the dish. Sit a pie funnel into the centre of the filling; it will support the pastry and stop it from sinking into the filling and becoming soggy.

Place the pastry lid over the top and press down on to the edges to seal. Trim off any excess pastry and crimp the edges with a fork, or between your thumb and forefinger. Brush the top with beaten egg and make a hole in the centre to reveal the pie funnel. Bake for 30–35 minutes until the pastry is crisp and golden.

meat and potato pie

This has got to be the definitive pie – loved or hated, it is eaten up and down the country as a ready-made hand-held pie or as a tray-baked school dinner. When made with good-quality minced steak and the right mixture of flavourings and pastry, it is delicious and one of the truly great pies. It requires a large amount of pastry as it is a double-crusted pie. My recipe is in the tray-baked family tradition; serve it with extra gravy, peas and mashed potato for the ultimate dinner (*illustrated on preceding pages*).

serves 6

for the pastry
500g/1lb shortcrust pastry (see page 15) · 2 tbsp milk, to glaze

for the filling
1 tbsp olive oil · 1 onion, finely chopped · 1 clove garlic, crushed · 700g/1¹/₂lb good-quality coarse-minced beef · 2 tbsp plain flour · 200ml/7fl oz beef stock · 2 tbsp tomato purée
2 tbsp HP brown sauce · 2 large potatoes, peeled and cubed · salt and ground black pepper

Preheat the oven to 200°C/400°F/Gas 6. Place a baking tray in the oven to heat.

Heat the oil in a large saucepan. Add the onion and cook gently for a few minutes until beginning to soften. Add the garlic and minced beef and cook for about 5 minutes until the meat is browned all over. Stir in the flour, toss with the beef and cook for a couple of minutes.

Add the beef stock, tomato purée, HP brown sauce and cubed potatoes and simmer gently for about 10 minutes until thickened slightly. Season well to taste and leave to cool.

Roll out half of the pastry and use to line a roasting tin or dish measuring 35 x 25cm/14 x 10in. Spoon the cooled filling mixture on to the pastry. Roll out the remaining pastry and place on top, pressing the edges together to seal. Crimp the edges using your fingertips and brush the top with a little milk to glaze. Place on the baking tray and bake for 35–40 minutes until golden.

free-form cheese, bacon and onion pie

This is a great throw-it-together pie. You don't need any special tin or pie dish and most of the ingredients are pretty much store-cupboard staples. So simple, but the most delicious thing served with a crisp salad and a sharp lemon dressing.

serves 4

for the pastry
500g/1lb ready-made puff pastry · beaten egg, to glaze

for the filling
2 large floury potatoes · 1 tbsp vegetable oil · 4 rashers smoked streaky bacon, cut into 2cm/^{3}/$_4$in strips · 2 large onions, thinly sliced · 200g/7oz mature Cheddar cheese, coarsely grated · 3 tbsp double cream · ground black pepper

Preheat the oven to 200°C/400°F/Gas 6.

Place the potatoes in a saucepan and cover with cold water. Bring to the boil and cook for 10–15 minutes until the potatoes are tender. Drain and, when cool enough to handle, cut the potatoes into thin slices. Heat the oil in a large frying pan and cook the bacon, stirring occasionally, for 2 minutes until beginning to colour. Add the onions and cook for 4–5 minutes until softened but not coloured. Set aside to cool.

Divide the pastry into two portions. Roll out one half to form a 25cm/10in square. Lay the pastry square on a lightly greased baking tray and brush the edges lightly with beaten egg. Spread the sliced potatoes over the pastry, then top with the bacon and onions, leaving a 2.5cm/1in border all the way around. Sprinkle with the grated cheese and season with ground black pepper. Drizzle over the cream.

Roll out the second piece of pastry to form a 28cm/11in square. Place over the filling and press the edges together to join. Trim away any excess and cut a cross in the middle of the pie. Brush lightly with beaten egg and bake in the top of the oven for 10 minutes, then reduce the heat to 180°C/350°F/Gas 4 and cook for a further 25–30 minutes, or until golden and risen.

Serve cut into wedges.

lamb, mint and pumpkin pie

What a wonderful pie – a perfect combination of flavours topped with toasted cumin pastry.

serves 6

for the pastry
400g/13oz shortcrust pastry (see page 15), with 2 tsp toasted cumin seeds added to the mixture · beaten egg, to glaze

for the filling
4 tbsp olive oil · 1kg/2lb boned shoulder of lamb, trimmed and cut into 2.5cm/1in cubes · 500ml/17fl oz brown ale, such as Old Speckled Hen · 2 large onions, chopped · 2 cloves garlic, chopped · 2 celery sticks, chopped · 2 bay leaves large bunch mint, chopped · 2 x 400g/13oz cans chopped tomatoes · 1 large red chilli · 1 large butternut squash, peeled and chopped into 2.5cm/1in cubes · salt and ground black pepper

Preheat the oven to 180°C/350°F/Gas 4.

Heat the olive oil in a 2 litre/3½ pint heavy-based flameproof casserole dish and fry the lamb until browned all over. Add the ale, onions, garlic, celery and bay, half the bunch of mint, the canned tomatoes and red chilli. Season well to taste and cover. Place in the oven to bake for 1½ hours. Add the butternut squash and continue to cook for a further 1 hour until the meat is very tender. Using a vegetable masher, press the butternut squash and mash it into the sauce to make a thick gravy with the tender lamb. Stir in the remaining mint, spoon into a 2 litre/3½ pint deep pie dish and leave to cool.

Increase the oven temperature to 200°C/400°F/Gas 6.

Roll out the pastry to a thickness of about 3mm/⅛in. Cut a 2cm/¾in strip from the rolled-out pastry. Brush the rim of the pie dish with water and place the pastry strip around the rim, pressing it down. Cut out a lid from the remaining pastry about 2.5cm/1in larger than the dish. Sit a pie funnel into the centre of the filling to support the pastry and stop it from sinking into the filling and becoming soggy. Place the pastry lid over the top and press down on to the edges to seal. Trim off any excess pastry and crimp the edges with a fork, or between your thumb and forefinger. Brush the pastry with beaten egg and make a hole in the centre to reveal the pie funnel. Use the pastry trimmings to make decorations for the top of the pie. Bake for 30–35 minutes until the pastry is crisp and golden.

game pie

As game meat can be quite unpredictable in its tenderness (which affects its cooking time), I poach the pheasant before adding it to the pie because this ensures that the meat is perfectly succulent. Also, you then have the wonderful game stock which can be used to make the delicious sauce for the pie. This is another special-occasion pie which deserves a perfect crust.

serves 6

for the pastry
400g/13oz rough puff pastry (see page 20) · beaten egg, to glaze

for the filling

4 pheasants · 3 onions · 1 carrot · 2 celery sticks · 4 black peppercorns · 25g/1oz plain flour
225g/7¹/₂oz lean stewing steak, cut into 2cm/³/₄in cubes · 100g/3¹/₂oz smoked streaky bacon,
cut into strips · 25g/1oz butter · 1 large clove garlic, finely chopped · 1 tbsp tomato purée
small bunch chopped parsley · 2 tbsp redcurrant jelly · 100g/3¹/₂oz chestnut mushrooms, sliced
small pinch grated nutmeg · salt and ground black pepper

Place the pheasants in a large saucepan and cover with water. Add 1 of the onions (whole), carrot
and celery and peppercorns and bring to the boil. Simmer for 1 hour or until the pheasants are
tender. Remove the pheasants from the stock and leave to cool. Return the stock to the hob and
continue to simmer until reduced by half, then set aside. Remove the pheasant meat from the
carcasses and chop roughly.

Place the flour in a bowl with some salt and black pepper. Add the stewing steak and toss well to
coat it in the flour.

Heat a heavy frying pan and cook the bacon for a few minutes until it releases its fat. Add the butter
and when it has melted add the stewing steak and cook for about 4 minutes until browned all over.
Chop the remaining onions and add to the pan with the garlic. Cook for a further few minutes, then
pour in 300ml/¹/₂ pint of the reduced pheasant stock. Add the tomato purée, parsley, redcurrant jelly
and the mushrooms. Season to taste and add the nutmeg. Cover and simmer gently for 30 minutes.
Add the chopped pheasant to the pan, then transfer to a 2 litre/3¹/₂ pint deep pie dish and set
aside to cool.

Preheat the oven to 200°C/400°F/Gas 6.

Roll out the pastry to a thickness of about 3mm/¹/₈in. Cut a 2cm/³/₄in strip from the rolled-out
pastry. Brush the rim of the pie dish with water and place the pastry strip around the rim, pressing
it down. Cut out a lid from the remaining pastry about 2.5cm/1in larger than the dish. Sit a pie
funnel into the centre of the filling to support the pastry and stop it from sinking into the filling and
becoming soggy. Place the pastry lid over the top and press down on the edges to seal. Trim off any
excess pastry and crimp the edges with a fork, or between your thumb and forefinger. Brush the top
with beaten egg and make a hole in the centre to reveal the pie funnel. Use the pastry trimmings to
make decorations for the top of the pie.

Bake for 30–35 minutes until the pastry is crisp and golden.

deep egg and bacon pie

This is rather like the classic quiche Lorraine with a pastry lid. You really can't go wrong with the combination of egg, bacon, cheese and onion. This deep pie is cooked in a loose-bottomed cake tin so it can be easily cut into wedges, making it perfect for picnics. I have no problem eating it for breakfast, though!

serves 6

for the pastry
400g/13oz rich shortcrust pastry (see page 16) · beaten egg, to glaze

for the filling
300g/10oz lean pork, such as loin · 200g/7oz smoked streaky bacon, derinded
1 tbsp olive oil · 1 large onion, finely chopped · 225g/7¹/₂oz mature Cheddar cheese, grated
1 clove garlic, crushed · bunch flat-leaf parsley, chopped roughly · bunch chives, chopped
2 eggs, lightly beaten · 4 tbsp crème fraîche · salt and ground black pepper

Preheat the oven to 180°C/350°F/Gas 4.

Finely chop the pork and bacon and mix together. This can be done easily in a food processor but be careful not to over-mince as the mixture can become too smooth. Heat the oil in a large saucepan and cook the onion for a few minutes. Add the pork and bacon and cook for about 5 minutes until lightly coloured. Transfer to a bowl and leave to cool, then stir in the remaining ingredients, seasoning with a little salt and plenty of ground black pepper.

Roll out two-thirds of the pastry to a disc measuring about 30cm/12in across and drape into a 22cm/8¹/₂in loose-bottomed cake tin to cover the bottom and the sides. Transfer the filling into the pie and brush the edges of the pastry with a little beaten egg. Roll out the remaining pastry to a smaller disc measuring 24cm/9¹/₂in across and place over the top of the filled pie, pressing the edges together to seal. Trim away any excess pastry and brush the top of the pie with the rest of the beaten egg. Pierce the top with a fork to allow steam to escape. Place on a baking sheet and bake for 50–60 minutes until golden and crisp.

Allow to cool for about 10 minutes before removing it from the tin. Serve cut into wedges.

sausage, apple and sage plate pie

Go to town with some
really top-quality sausages to
make this pie. With so many
good ones now available,
you shouldn't go wrong.
I use a fine Cumberland
sausage for this as it doesn't
have an overpowering
flavour and works well with
the apple and sage. Cook
this pie in a shallow metal
dish to ensure the base
stays crispy.

serves 4

for the pastry
300g/10oz shortcrust pastry (see page 15) · beaten egg, to glaze

for the filling
450g/14¹/₂oz good-quality Cumberland sausages · 2 tbsp olive oil · 2 onions, finely sliced
1 tbsp wholegrain mustard · 1 tbsp chopped fresh sage · 2 small apples, peeled, cored and
chopped · 2 tbsp crème fraîche · salt and ground black pepper

Preheat the oven to 200°C/400°F/Gas 6.

Roll out about 175g/6oz of the pastry and use to line a shallow 23cm/9in pie plate or dish.
Roll out the remaining pastry about 2cm/³/₄in bigger than the pie plate and set aside.

Split the sausages, remove the skin and break up the meat into small pieces. Heat the oil in a large
frying pan and gently cook the onions for about 8–10 minutes until softened. Add the sausage meat
and cook for a further 5 minutes, stirring frequently until browned all over and breaking up the
sausages further with a wooden spoon during cooking. Remove from the heat and add the mustard,
sage, chopped apples and crème fraîche. Season with a little salt and ground black pepper and mix
well. Leave to cool.

Once the mixture has cooled, pile it into the centre of the pie plate. Brush the edges of the pastry
with beaten egg and then top with the rolled-out lid, sealing the edges by pressing down well.
Trim off any excess pastry and crimp the edges with a fork, or between your thumb and forefinger.
Brush with the remaining egg and make a hole or several slashes in the top to release the steam.
Bake for 25–30 minutes until the pastry is golden brown.

beef wellington

This pie is really one to go to town on with your pastry techniques. It is not necessarily a true pie, but in keeping with my definition of 'any filling wrapped in pastry' it certainly fits the bill.

The method of cooking meat wrapped in pastry has a history that goes back to the eighteenth century and is a variation on the French classic *boeuf en croûte*. The English name was applied in 1815 in honour of the Duke of Wellington.

serves 6

for the pastry
500g/1lb ready-made puff pastry · beaten egg, to glaze

for the filling
25g/1oz butter · 1 onion, finely chopped · 150g/5oz chestnut mushrooms, finely chopped
2 cloves garlic, finely chopped · 3 tbsp chopped flat-leaf parsley · 100g/3¹/₂oz smooth liver pâté
750g/1¹/₂lb beef fillet · salt and ground black pepper

Melt the butter in a large frying pan and cook the onion for about 5 minutes until beginning to soften. Add the mushrooms and cook for a further 5 minutes until soft and creamy. Stir in the garlic and parsley and season with a little salt and plenty of ground black pepper. Set aside to cool.

Beat the pâté into the mushroom mixture and set aside.

Preheat the oven to 200°C/400°F/Gas 6.

Roll out the puff pastry on a lightly floured surface to a sheet large enough to enclose the beef, reserving the offcuts for decoration. Spread the pâté mixture down the middle of the pastry and lay the beef on top of the mixture. Brush the edges of the pastry with beaten egg and fold the pastry over the meat to enclose it in a neat parcel, sealing the edges well. Place the meat parcel on to a baking sheet, seam side down. Cut decorative leaves from the reserved pastry. Brush the parcel with beaten egg, decorate with the leaves and chill for about 10 minutes.

Bake for 40–45 minutes until the pastry is golden and puffed up. Transfer to a serving board and leave to stand for 10 minutes. Serve cut into thick slices.

russian fish pie

A Victorian and Edwardian favourite, this pie was adopted by the British from a Russian original known as *coulibiac*. Despite the fact that it has a pastry crust and is served hot, it resembles another famous import – kedgeree.

serves 6

for the pastry
500g/1lb ready-made puff pastry · beaten egg, to glaze

for the filling
450g/14¹/₂oz salmon fillet · 300ml/¹/₂ pint milk · 3 black peppercorns · 1 bay leaf
100g/3¹/₂oz long-grain rice · 25g/1oz butter · 1 onion, finely chopped · 100g/3¹/₂oz mushrooms, thinly sliced · 4 hard-boiled eggs, sliced · pinch cayenne pepper · 2 tbsp chopped flat-leaf parsley
grated zest and juice 1 small lemon

Preheat the oven to 220°C/425°F/Gas 7.

Place the salmon in a large frying pan with the milk, peppercorns and bay leaf. Poach gently for about 5 minutes until the salmon is cooked through and flakes easily. Remove the salmon from the pan and allow to cool; discard the milk.

Place the rice in a large saucepan of boiling water and cook for 10–12 minutes until tender. Drain and set aside. Heat the butter in a large saucepan and cook the onion for 5–6 minutes until tender. Add the mushrooms and cook for a further 5 minutes.

Place the cooked rice in a bowl and stir through the onion, mushrooms, hard-boiled eggs, cayenne pepper, parsley, salmon, lemon zest and juice and plenty of salt and ground black pepper.

Roll out the pastry to 40cm/16in square. Pile the filling in the centre. Wet the corners of the pastry and fold them upwards so that they meet and overlap slightly in the centre to make an envelope shape. Press the joins together firmly and brush the pie all over with beaten egg.

Place on a large baking tray and bake for 35–40 minutes until golden and puffed up.

the pie and mash shop

Eels, pie and mash are a combination particularly associated with London. Just after World War II, it was possible to consume pie and mash in at least 130 shops scattered all over the city. Today, only a fraction of the original eel, pie and mash houses remain and the majority are now situated in London's East End. Many people therefore believe this dish is an East End tradition.

The story begins in Victorian England, where the bustling streets were populated by piemen who walked miles each day selling meat, fish and fruit

pies. These piemen provided many poor families with their only opportunity to buy hot food at a reasonable price. The meat pies were usually made from mutton or beef, the fruit pies consisted of apples, damsons, cherries and currants and the fish pies were filled with eels.

Eels had become a popular dish for Londoners. They were usually accompanied by pea soup or parsley sauce, with chillies and vinegar added for spice. This parsley sauce is the famous 'liquor' that is still served today. It is a basic recipe consisting of a thin white sauce with chopped parsley stirred in.

The first pie and mash shop was recorded in the late 1800s. It would have sold a variety of meat, eel and fruit pies, live eels, pea soup and mashed potato. These shops heralded the end of the street piemen. A typical shop was fitted out with marble tables, wooden benches, white-tiled walls and huge mirrors. Today, it is always an experience to dine in one of the few remaining outlets, which retain their original grandeur and are steeped in tradition and history. Even in cosmopolitan and ever-changing London, it is heartening that the pie and mash shop has managed to resist total obsolescence and you can still buy a very tasty home-made pie served with mash and gravy or liquor for a very reasonable price – a fact that will hopefully ensure the future of eels, pie and mash.

chicken, leek and tarragon pie

It's difficult to single out the best chicken pie, but after many tried-and-tested combinations this has got to be my favourite. The tarragon and lemon provide a lovely touch of freshness.

serves 4–6

for the pastry
400g/13oz rich shortcrust pastry (see page 16) · beaten egg, to glaze

for the filling
1.5kg/3lb free-range chicken · 1 carrot, roughly chopped · 2 celery sticks, roughly chopped
2 onions, finely chopped · 4 sprigs tarragon · 1 tbsp olive oil · knob of butter
2 leeks, finely sliced · 150ml/^{1}/4 pint white wine · 2 tbsp plain flour · 150ml/^{1}/4 pint single cream
grated zest of ^{1}/2 lemon · salt and ground black pepper

Place the chicken in a large saucepan with the carrot, celery, 1 of the onions and 3 tarragon sprigs. Season with a little salt and pepper and cover with water. Bring to the boil and simmer for 45 minutes until the chicken is cooked through. Remove the chicken from the pan and set aside to cool. Return the stock to the hob and simmer gently for a further 30 minutes until it is reduced by half.

Meanwhile heat the oil and butter in a large frying pan, add the leeks and the remaining onion and gently cook for about 5 minutes until softened. Turn up the heat to high, add the wine and simmer rapidly for 3–4 minutes until reduced by half. Stir in the flour and mix well in the pan for 1 minute. Pour in the cream, about 150ml/^{1}/4 pint of the reduced chicken stock and the lemon zest. Season with a little salt and plenty of ground black pepper.

Remove the meat from the cooled chicken carcass and chop or shred into small pieces. Add this and the remaining tarragon, chopped, to the leek and cream mixture and stir together. Set aside to cool.

Preheat the oven to 180°C/350°F/Gas 4. Place a baking tray in the oven to heat.

Line the base of a 30 x 20cm/12 x 8in rectangular or 26cm/10^1/2in round pie tin with two-thirds of the pastry and fill with the chicken mixture. Brush the pastry edges with beaten egg. Roll out the remaining pastry to make a lid and lay over the filling, crimping the edges of the pastry with your fingertips to seal. Trim away any excess and brush with beaten egg to glaze. Place on the baking tray and bake for 30–35 minutes until the pastry is golden and crisp.

chicken, lemon and oregano pie cooked in a frying pan

The filling for this pie is based on *avgolemono*, a Greek sauce which is made from eggs and lemon. The recipe comes from my pal and fellow food writer Silvana Franco. She tops it with an oregano pastry, but if you are a bit pushed for time, ready-made shortcrust will do just fine.

serves 6

for the pastry
300g/10oz shortcrust pastry (see page 15), with 1 tbsp dried oregano added to the dry mixture

for the filling
8 skinless, boneless chicken thighs, cut into 2.5cm/1in cubes · 1 tbsp plain flour · 2 tbsp olive oil, plus extra to glaze · 70g/2¹/₂oz pancetta, cubed · 2 large potatoes, peeled and cut into 2cm/³/₄in dice · 1 large onion, thinly sliced · 3 large egg yolks · grated zest and juice 3 lemons 450ml/³/₄ pint warm chicken stock · 4 tbsp chopped fresh mint · salt and ground black pepper

Preheat the oven to 190°C/375°F/Gas 5.

Dust the chicken in the flour, shaking off the excess. Heat the oil in a 24cm/9¹/₂in heavy-based frying pan or oven- and flameproof dish. Add the chicken and pancetta and cook for about 5 minutes over a high heat until the chicken is nicely browned. Lift out the chicken and pancetta with a slotted spoon and set aside. Lower the heat, add the potatoes and onion and cook gently for 5–8 minutes until the onion is softened and golden.

In a large bowl, whisk together the egg yolks, lemon zest and lemon juice. Slowly pour in the hot chicken stock, stirring continuously until the sauce is foamy and has thickened slightly. Season with salt and freshly ground pepper, then stir in the mint. Take the pan off the heat and stir in the browned chicken and pancetta and the lemon sauce.

Roll out the pastry on a floured surface to make a circle a bit bigger than the pan. Lay it on top of the pan, roughly tucking the edges down the side of the pan. Brush the top with olive oil and bake in the oven for 25–30 minutes until the pastry is dark golden.

greek spinach pie

This famous spinach and feta pie (*spanokopita*) is something so simple and sublime that I had to include it in the book. It looks tricky but, believe me, it really is straightforward to prepare – especially as wafer-thin filo pastry is widely available now. You may find that shop-bought filo comes in various sizes, so adapt the recipe to fit.

serves 4

for the pastry
8 sheets ready-made filo pastry, measuring 25 x 23cm/10 x 9in

for the filling
500g/1lb spinach · 100g/3¹/₂oz butter · 1 large onion, finely chopped · 2 cloves garlic, chopped
200g/7oz feta cheese, crumbled · 2 tbsp pine nuts, toasted · 2 eggs, beaten
2 tbsp chopped fresh dill · 4 tbsp chopped flat-leaf parsley · salt and ground black pepper

Preheat the oven to 180°C/350°F/Gas 4.

Wash the spinach well, if it is not prewashed. Place it in a large saucepan over a low heat to cook down gently until completely wilted. Leave to cool, then drain well and squeeze out any excess liquid using your hands. Chop roughly.

Melt about 25g/1oz of the butter in a frying pan, add the onion and cook for about 5 minutes until beginning to soften. Stir in the garlic and cook for a further minute. Remove from the heat and in a large bowl combine the onion and garlic with the spinach, cheese, pine nuts, eggs, herbs and seasoning to taste.

Melt the remaining butter. Arrange a sheet of filo pastry in the base of a shallow tin or ovenproof dish measuring about 22cm/8¹/₂in square, allowing the edges of the pastry to overhang. Brush with melted butter, then arrange 3 more sheets on top, brushing each sheet as you go. Spoon the filling on top and spread out evenly. Fold the edges of the filo on to the spinach filling. Place another layer of filo pastry on top of the spinach mixture and brush with melted butter. Arrange 3 more sheets of pastry on top, brushing each sheet as you go. Score the top lightly into squares and then bake for 20–25 minutes until golden brown. Serve hot or cold.

A very simple shortcrust pastry flavoured and streaked with saffron strands. Beautiful and delicious too.

spanish pepper and chorizo pie

This is a hearty, family-sized pie, known as *empanada gallega*, which is eaten all over Spain in many variations. Its most popular fillings are always chorizo sausage, cured ham and pork with red peppers and onions.

   The pastry crust is traditionally more like a pizza dough, but I have adapted it and topped the pie with a very simple shortcrust pastry streaked with saffron strands. It's a truly flavoursome pie and needs little accompaniment – just serve on its own with cold beers (*illustrated on preceding page*).

serves 6

for the pastry
200g/7oz plain flour · 1/4 tsp salt · 100g/3¹/2oz cold unsalted butter, cubed · 2 egg yolks, beaten
2 tbsp iced water · pinch saffron strands

for the filling
25g/1oz butter · 2 large onions, chopped · 1 red pepper, seeded and chopped
1 green pepper, seeded and chopped · 1 small hot red chilli, seeded and finely chopped
1 clove garlic, finely chopped · small bunch flat-leaf parsley, chopped · 300g/10oz chorizo
sausage, diced · 250g/8oz lean pork loin, finely diced · 90g/3¹/4oz cured Serrano ham
salt and ground black pepper

For the pastry, place the flour and salt in a bowl and add the cubes of cold butter. Gently and swiftly rub the fat into the flour, using your fingertips, until it resembles coarse crumbs. Make a well in the centre of the dry ingredients. Mix the egg yolks with the iced water and saffron strands. Reserving a little for glazing the pie, gradually add the egg mixture to the dry ingredients, a little at a time, using a knife to mix the dough as you go. Turn out the dough on to a floured surface and knead lightly until smooth. Shape into a ball, wrap in cling film and leave to rest in the fridge until you have prepared the filling.

Heat the butter in a large frying pan and cook the onions gently for about 10 minutes until softened. Add the red and green peppers, chilli and garlic and cook for a further 15 minutes until softened. Stir in the chopped parsley and season with a little salt and pepper to taste.

Preheat the oven to 180°C/350°F/Gas 4.

Roll out two-thirds of the pastry on a lightly floured surface to fit a 23cm/9in pie dish.

Mix the chorizo and pork into the pepper mixture and spoon into the pie shell. Lay the slices of
Serrano ham on top. Brush the edges of the pastry with beaten egg mixture.

Roll out the remaining pastry to make a lid and lay it on top of the pie. Trim off any excess and crimp
the edges between your finger and forefinger. Make 3 small slashes in the top to release the steam.
Brush the top with the remaining egg and saffron mixture and bake in the oven for 50 minutes until
golden. Leave to stand for a good 30 minutes to let everything settle before serving it in wedges.

vegetable and rice picnic pie

This was a pie my mother used to make regularly for snacks, school lunchboxes or for picnics. Rice cakes, or *torta* as they are known in Italy, are found with a multitude of flavourings, including ham, cheese, herbs and vegetables. The uncooked rice cooks perfectly inside the pastry crust, giving a tasty, creamy filling which is sturdy enough to travel and to eat on the go.

serves 4–6

for the pastry
300g/10oz plain flour · pinch salt · 150ml/1/4 pint water · 1 tsp olive oil · 2 tbsp milk, to glaze

for the filling
500g/1lb spinach · 300g/10oz courgettes, thinly sliced · 1 onion, thinly sliced
100g/3¹/₂oz risotto rice · 50g/2oz Parmesan cheese, grated · 2 eggs, beaten, plus 1 extra to glaze
1 tsp sea salt · salt and ground black pepper

To make the pastry, put the flour and salt in a bowl, then stir in the water and oil to make a smooth, firm dough. Cover with a damp cloth and leave to rest for at least 10 minutes.

Preheat the oven to 180°C/350°F/Gas 4.

Wash the spinach well and place in a large saucepan with just the water that clings to its leaves. Cook for 5 minutes until wilted completely. Leave to cool, then squeeze out any excess water and chop roughly.

In a large bowl, mix the spinach, courgettes, onion, rice, Parmesan, eggs and a little salt and pepper.

Halve the pastry and roll out each piece to 5mm/1/4in thick. Use one half to line an oiled 20 x 30cm/8 x 12in Swiss roll tin. Spoon in the filling, then cover with the remaining pastry. Trim the edges and press together to seal. To glaze, mix the remaining egg and milk and brush this on the pie lid, then sprinkle with sea salt. Bake for 40 minutes until golden brown. Serve warm or cold, cut into squares.

stargazy pie

This very famous pie from Cornwall was originally made using pilchards and herrings. The fish were usually arranged so that their heads peeped out of a hole in the centre of the pastry and they appeared to be gazing skyward. Although very dramatic, it is not the most practical of pies for eating. My version here uses fillets of mackerel, which still makes for a very tasty pie without changing the original ingredients combination too much (*illustrated on preceding pages*).

serves 4

for the pastry
300g/10oz shortcrust pastry (see page 15)

for the filling
15g/¹/₂oz butter · 50g/2oz breadcrumbs · 2 large potatoes, peeled, parboiled and thinly sliced
2 rashers bacon, chopped · 2 tbsp chopped chives · 2 tbsp chopped flat-leaf parsley
4 fillets of mackerel · 3 eggs, beaten, plus I extra to glaze · 150ml/¹/₄ pint double cream
salt and ground black pepper

Preheat the oven to 200°C/400°F/Gas 6.

Butter a 23cm/9in deep pie dish and sprinkle with breadcrumbs so that they stick to the sides. Arrange the potatoes in the base of the dish and sprinkle with half of the bacon and half of the chives and parsley. Season with a little salt and ground black pepper.

Lay the mackerel fillets on top and sprinkle with the remaining bacon, chives, parsley and seasoning. Beat the eggs together with the cream and pour this over the fish.

Roll out the pastry to a thickness of about 3mm/¹/₈in. Cut a 2cm/³/₄in strip from the rolled-out pastry. Brush the rim of the pie dish with water and place the pastry strip around the rim, pressing it down. Cut out a lid from the remaining pastry about 2.5cm/1in larger than the dish. Arrange a pie funnel in the centre of the pie and place the pastry lid on top, pressing down to seal the edges. Trim off any excess pastry and crimp the edges with a fork, or between your thumb and forefinger. Brush the top with beaten egg and bake for 10 minutes, then reduce the temperature to 180°C/350°F/Gas 4 and bake for a further 20 minutes until the pastry is crisp and golden and the filling is set. Serve hot with boiled new potatoes tossed in chopped fresh parsley.

the gourmet pie shop

Things have really come a long way since the days of the basic pie and mash shop and the take-away pie from the chippy. We are now seeing the emergence of stylish, gourmet pie restaurants and a new generation of pie makers who are putting pies firmly back in favour. Selling delicious pies with sophisticated fillings and superb pastry alongside salads, creamy mash and vegetables makes for a whole new dining experience.

Meeting Andrew Fisher and Luke Bryan, who run Pokeno Pies in Brighton, was an insight into true pie passion. Inspired by the wonderful gourmet pies of Australia and New Zealand, they wanted to bring the same levels of quality and enthusiasm to Britain. British pies had developed a bit of an image problem, with the popular perception that they were cheap and bad for you. But it doesn't have to be that way, says Andrew. If people love gourmet pies in the heat of Oz, they should adore them all year round in Britain.

After months of research and tasting, the Pokeno Pies café bar was launched. (Pokeno is the name of a town in New Zealand on their research trail.) A strong manifesto states that the pies are hand-made using high-quality natural ingredients, sourced locally, with no artificial preservatives, flavour enhancers, colourants or hydrogenated fats and are topped with their own special pastry, made with butter from a local Sussex farm. It just shows how far we've moved away from the horrors of mass-produced pies, where caramel and E numbers are added instead of browning the meat and flavourless palm fat is added to the pastry instead of butter.

Pokeno pies are heaped high with fragrant fillings including chicken and butternut squash, minted lamb and potato, Moroccan aubergine and feta and, my favourite, steak, chorizo and olive. These are not any old pies and, given their recent accolades, the critics seem to have noticed too. Who could ever have imagined that the humble pie would one day be enjoyed whilst sipping a smooth Merlot or an organic ale?

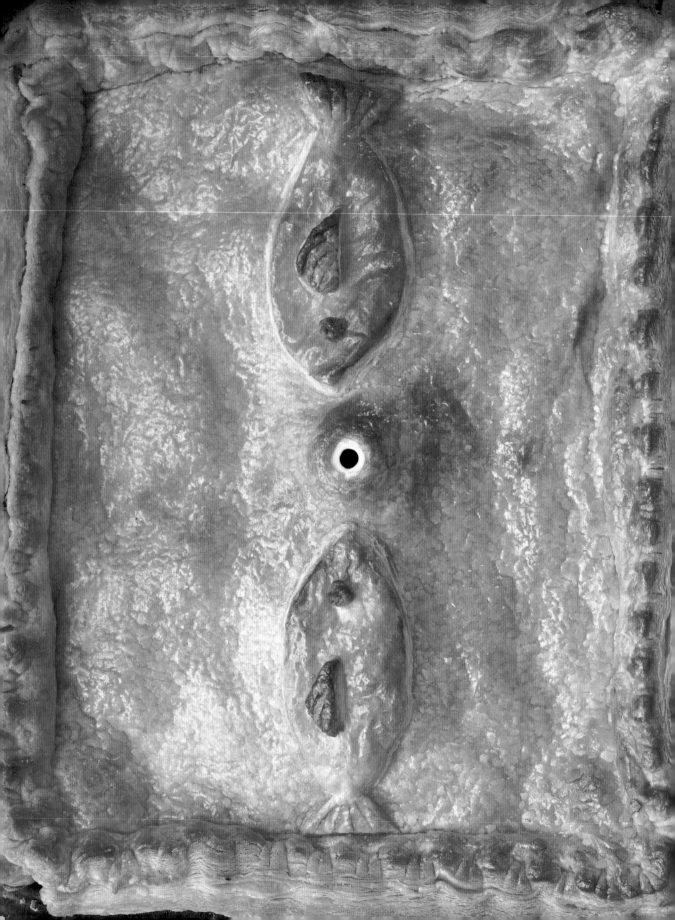

smoked fish and cider pie

A pie book would not be complete without a fish pie. I chose this classic as it's simple and delicious but has a wonderful flavour from the mixture of smoked fish and cider.

serves 4

for the pastry
375g/12oz ready-rolled puff pastry · beaten egg, to glaze

for the filling
450g/14¹/₂oz fresh haddock fillet, skinned · 125g/4oz smoked haddock fillet, skinned
1 large potato, peeled, parboiled and finely sliced · 40g/1¹/₂oz butter · 1 onion, finely chopped
50g/2oz plain flour · 400ml/14fl oz dry cider · 3 tbsp crème fraîche · 75g/3oz frozen peas
2 tbsp chopped fresh parsley · 250g/8oz medium raw prawns · salt and ground black pepper

Preheat the oven to 200°C/400°F/Gas 6.

Cut the fresh and smoked haddock into 2.5cm/1in pieces. Lay the parboiled potato in the base of a 1.5 litre/2¹/₂ pint pie dish. Heat the butter in a medium saucepan until melted and foaming. Add the onion and cook for 5 minutes until softened. Add the flour and cook for a few minutes until it forms a smooth paste. Gradually pour the cider into the pan, stirring constantly with a wooden spoon until you have a smooth thickened sauce. Remove from the heat and stir in the crème fraîche. Season with a little salt and plenty of ground black pepper, then stir in the peas, parsley, prawns and haddock pieces. Spoon the mixture into the pie dish on top of the potato.

Moisten the edges of the dish with a little water and place a pie funnel in the centre of the filling. Unroll the pastry and lay it on top. Brush with the egg and bake for 35–40 minutes until golden.

cheshire cheese and onion pie

I have crossed counties by mixing flavoursome red Leicester cheese in the pastry of this pie with creamy Cheshire cheese in the filling. It really works to give a moreish, delicious pie which is simplicity itself. The sliced potatoes cook in the steam generated inside the pie (saving you the job of precooking them), so don't be tempted to put a steam hole in the pastry.

serves 4

for the pastry
300g/10oz cheese pastry (see page 17), made with red Leicester cheese · 2 tbsp milk, to glaze

for the filling
1 bunch spring onions, roughly chopped · 125g/4oz Cheshire cheese, crumbled
4 tbsp crème fraîche · 1 bunch chives, snipped · 500g/1lb floury potatoes, such as Estima or Maris Piper, peeled and very thinly sliced · salt and ground black pepper

Preheat the oven to 180°C/350°F/Gas 4.

Roll out about 175g/6oz of the pastry on a lightly floured surface and line a 23cm/9in shallow pie dish. Mix together the spring onions, Cheshire cheese, crème fraîche and snipped chives in a small bowl, seasoning with a little salt and plenty of ground black pepper.

Arrange the potatoes in layers with a few tablespoons of the spring onion and cheese mixture spread between each layer. Continue until all the potatoes and cheese mixture are used up. Brush the edge of the pastry with a little milk.

Roll out the remaining pastry about 2cm/³/4in larger than the dish and then lay this over the top of the pie. Crimp the edges to seal and brush with a little milk to glaze, then bake for approximately 30 minutes.

Reduce the temperature to 160°C/325°F/Gas 3 and cook for a further 40 minutes until the pastry is golden and the potatoes are cooked through. To test if the potatoes are cooked, simply insert a skewer into the pie and test for tenderness.

If the pastry is cooking too quickly, place a loose piece of foil over the top.

Leave to cool slightly before serving so that the filling melds together perfectly. This will make it easier to slice and to serve in wedges.

fidget pie

This is a lovely old-fashioned recipe from Shropshire, traditionally served to the workers during harvest time. The name of this pie is said to have come from the fact that it was originally 'fitched' or five-sided in shape. I just love the name of it and the combination of ingredients in the filling. Apples and gammon are perfect partners.

serves 4

for the pastry
300g/10oz shortcrust pastry (see page 15) · milk or beaten egg, to glaze

for the filling
40g/1¹/2oz butter · 3 medium potatoes, peeled and finely sliced · 2 onions, sliced
2 cooking apples, peeled, cored and sliced (weighing about 350g/11¹/2oz prepared weight)
2 tsp finely chopped sage · 2 tsp light muscovado sugar · 3 slices sweetcure gammon, de-rinded and cut into 1cm/¹/2in strips · 150ml/¹/4 pint vegetable stock · salt and ground black pepper

Preheat the oven to 180°C/350°F/Gas 4.

Heat the butter in a large frying pan and gently cook the potatoes, onions and apples in the butter until just golden. Stir in the sage. Transfer the potatoes, onions and apples to a 1 litre/1³/4 pint pie dish, sprinkle on the sugar and season with salt and pepper.

Place the gammon in the frying pan and cook lightly in the remaining fat until golden, then add to the pie dish. Pour over the stock.

On a lightly floured surface, roll out the pastry to a thickness of about 3mm/¹/8in and cover the pie, trimming the edges. Make a steam hole and decorate with the trimmings. Brush with milk or egg.

Bake for 30 minutes, then reduce the heat of the oven to 160°C/325°F/Gas 3 for a further 10–15 minutes until the pie is golden brown.

cornmeal crust chilli pie

The crusty cornmeal pastry of this pie soaks up the juices from the chilli and also helps to concentrate the flavours of the filling during baking.

serves 4–6

for the pastry
300g/10oz shortcrust pastry (see page 15), 50g/2oz of the flour replaced with coarse yellow cornmeal or polenta · beaten egg, to glaze

for the filling
2 tbsp sunflower oil · 1 large onion, finely chopped · 2 cloves garlic, finely chopped 1 tsp ground cumin · 1 tsp smoked paprika · 450g/14^1/2oz minced beef · 1 red pepper, deseeded and diced · 2 green chillies, chopped · 400g/13oz can chopped tomatoes 400g/13oz can chilli beans · salt and ground black pepper

Heat the oil in a large saucepan. Add the onion and garlic and cook for 5 minutes or until softened but not coloured. Add the cumin, paprika, minced beef, red pepper and chillies and cook for a further 5 minutes until lightly browned, breaking up any lumps of beef with a wooden spoon. Pour in the tomatoes and chilli beans, then season to taste. Bring to the boil, reduce the heat and simmer gently for 30 minutes or until the beef is tender and the sauce has slightly reduced. Spoon the mixture into a 1.5 litre/2^1/2 pint pie dish and leave to cool.

Preheat the oven to 200°C/400°F/Gas 6.

Roll out the pastry to a thickness of about 3mm/^{1}/8in. Cut a 2cm/^{3}/4in strip from the rolled-out pastry. Brush the rim of the pie dish with water and place the pastry strip around the rim, pressing it down. Cut out a lid from the remaining pastry about 2.5cm/1in larger than the dish.

Sit a pie funnel into the centre of the filling to support the pastry and stop it from sinking into the filling and becoming soggy. Place the pastry lid over the top of the dish and press down on the edges to seal. Trim off any excess pastry and crimp the edges with a fork, or between your thumb and forefinger. Brush with beaten egg and make a hole in the centre to reveal the pie funnel. Use the pastry trimmings to make decorations for the top of the pie. Bake for 30–35 minutes until the pastry is crisp and golden.

ham, leek and cider pan pie

This idea was taken from a traditional Lancashire pie recipe which ingeniously puts a light suet pastry lid on the pie filling while it is still in the pan and the whole pie is then cooked on the hob. The creamy ham and leek filling really works well with the tender pastry which soaks up all the juices. This method not only produces a pie that tastes fantastic and is easy to make but also saves on the all-important washing up.

serves 4

for the pastry
100g/3¹/₂oz plain flour · 50g/2oz vegetable suet, grated · pinch salt · ¹/₄ tsp baking powder

for the filling
25g/1oz butter · 2 large leeks, chopped · 900g/1³/₄lb unsmoked gammon joint, cut into 2.5cm/1in cubes · 2 carrots, peeled and roughly chopped · 3 celery sticks, finely sliced 1 large potato, peeled and chopped · handful fresh thyme leaves · 2 tbsp plain flour 400ml/14fl oz dry cider · 3 tbsp crème fraîche · salt and ground black pepper

Heat the butter in a large flameproof casserole dish and gently cook the leeks for a few minutes until beginning to soften. Add the cubed gammon, all the vegetables and the thyme and toss together well with the flour. Increase the heat, pour in the cider and bring to the boil. Reduce to a gentle simmer and stir through the crème fraîche. Season with a little salt and ground black pepper and simmer for 35 minutes until the meat is tender and the sauce thickened.

Meanwhile make the pastry by combining the flour, suet, salt and baking powder in a large bowl and mixing to a dough with about 2–3 tablespoons of water. On a lightly floured surface, roll out the pastry to 1cm/¹/₂in thick and lay it over the stew in the dish. Cover with a lid and simmer for 30 minutes until the pastry is puffed up and cooked through.

If you want to brown the top of the pastry to create a golden crust before serving, simply place the dish under a preheated grill for 3–4 minutes.

handpie

Small savoury pies really are little treasure chests of pure delight. They always look so perfect and enticing and make you just want to take a bite to reveal the secret of what lies within.

Cold hand-held pies are ideal for picnics and encasing them in crisp shortcrust pastry will make them sturdy enough to withstand a journey. Hot individual pies, served straight from the oven with tender, juicy meat and vegetable fillings, make the best small pies for dinner, served with mash and peas. Alternatively, you can use them as little savoury bites, served as a starter with drinks.

However you decide to enjoy them, the following recipes will suit any occasion and can be eaten without the aid of a plate – just hold your pie aloft and eat!

chicken and mushroom pies

These individual chicken and mushroom pies are made extra special by adding dried wild mushrooms and a splash of sherry and cream. Far grander than shop-bought versions, they are indulgent little pies that will certainly impress your friends. As you're already pulling out all the stops, experiment with some creative pastry decoration too.

makes 6 pies

for the pastry
400g/13oz rich shortcrust pastry (see page 16) · beaten egg, to glaze

for the filling
20g/³/₄oz dried wild mushrooms · 25g/1oz butter · 1 tbsp olive oil
1 large onion, finely chopped · 2 cloves garlic, chopped · 2 chicken thighs, skinned and cut into pieces
about 1.5cm/³/₄in square · 2 large chicken breasts, cut into pieces about 1.5cm/³/₄in square
250g/8oz chestnut mushrooms, sliced · 3 tbsp dry sherry or Marsala · 25g/1oz plain flour
2 tbsp double cream · small bunch flat-leaf parsley, roughly chopped

Place the dried mushrooms in a small bowl and cover with boiling water. Leave to soak for about
20 minutes. Drain the dried mushrooms, reserving 200ml/7fl oz of the soaking liquid. Strain the
reserved soaking liquid through a fine sieve to remove any gritty bits. Chop the mushrooms finely.

Meanwhile, heat the butter and oil in a large frying pan and gently cook the onion for about
5 minutes until softened and golden. Stir in the garlic, chicken and chestnut mushrooms and cook
on a high heat for a further 6 minutes. Add the sherry or Marsala and simmer rapidly for a minute.

Reduce the temperature to medium and stir in the flour until evenly mixed in. Add the drained dried
mushrooms and reserved soaking liquid. Simmer together for about 5 minutes, then add the cream
and cook for a further 5 minutes until the sauce is thickened. Stir in the parsley and season well to
taste. Set aside to cool.

Preheat the oven to 180°C/350°F/Gas 4.

Roll out the pastry and cut out 6 x 15cm/6in rounds to line
6 x 10cm/4in small individual pie tins. Press the pastry into the
bottom and up the sides of each tin, allowing a little overhang.
Fill each shell with the cooled filling and either cut out 6 x
10cm/4in rounds from the remaining pastry for lids or cut into
thick strips to make a lattice pastry top. Brush the tops with
beaten egg and bake for 30–35 minutes until golden. Leave the
pies in the tins to cool for about 5 minutes before removing.
Serve immediately.

mini pork and pancetta pies

These are the ultimate picnic pies – sturdy enough to withstand a journey and tasty enough to be devoured when you arrive, or maybe even on the way. They can be made up to 1 day ahead and are also a great choice for packed lunches, served with crunchy radishes and spring onions.

makes 12 pies

for the pastry
300g/10oz shortcrust pastry (see page 15) · beaten egg, to glaze

for the filling
1 bunch spring onions, finely chopped · pinch chilli flakes · 225g/8oz pork loin, finely chopped with a knife or in a food processor · 100g/3¹/₂oz pancetta, finely chopped
small bunch chives, snipped · small bunch parsley, finely chopped · salt and ground black pepper
12 quail's eggs, soft-boiled and peeled

Preheat the oven to 200°C/400°F/Gas 6.

For the filling, mix together all the ingredients except the quail's eggs in a large bowl, seasoning well to taste.

Roll out the pastry on a lightly floured surface and cut out 12 x 9cm/4in rounds to fit a 12-hole muffin tin and 12 x 7cm/3in rounds for the lids. Carefully press the larger rounds into the holes of the muffin tin. Half fill each with the pork filling, top with a soft-boiled quail's egg, then add another layer of filling.

Brush the edges of each pie with a little egg and then place a lid on top, pressing the edges together to seal. Make a hole in the top of each pie, brush the tops with egg to glaze and bake for 20 minutes. Reduce the oven temperature to 160°C/325°F/Gas 3 and cook for a further 25–30 minutes until the pastry is golden and the filling is cooked through. Leave to cool in the tin for 5 minutes before transferring to a wire rack to cool completely.

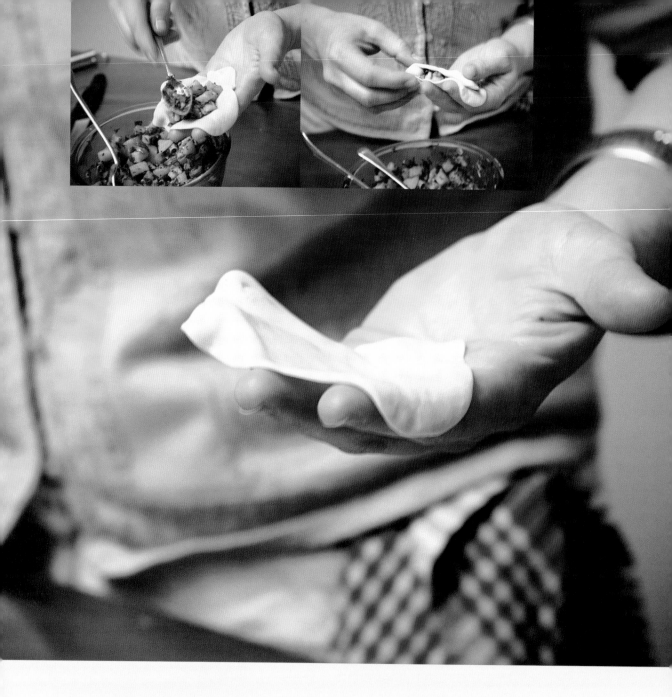

masala pasties

These tasty, spiced pasties were inspired by South Indian masala dosa pancakes, which have a potato, green chilli and onion filling. They are delicious served with a dipping sauce made from mango chutney, chopped coriander and lemon juice *(illustrated on preceding pages)*.

makes approximately 20

for the pastry
225g/8oz plain flour · 1/2 tsp salt · 2 tbsp vegetable oil

for the filling
600g/1 1/4lb potatoes, peeled and cut into 1.5cm/3/4in dice · 2 tbsp olive oil · 1/2 tsp cumin seeds
1/2 tsp black mustard seeds · 1/2 tsp garam masala · 1 green chilli, deseeded and finely chopped
2 cloves garlic, finely chopped · 6 spring onions, finely chopped · juice 1/2 lemon
small bunch fresh coriander, chopped · vegetable oil, for deep-frying

To make the pastry, place the flour and salt in a large mixing bowl. Add the oil and mix together, using your fingertips to rub it in. Once the oil and flour are combined, gradually mix in about 250ml/8fl oz of water, a little at a time, until you have a firm dough. Knead the dough for 5–7 minutes, until smooth. Form into a ball, brush with a little oil and set aside covered with either a damp cloth or cling film while you prepare the filling.

Place the potatoes in a saucepan and cover with water. Bring to the boil and simmer for 12–15 minutes until just tender but still holding their shape. Drain well.

Heat the olive oil in a large frying pan and gently heat the cumin seeds and mustard seeds until they begin to pop, then stir in the garam masala. Add the drained potatoes to the pan and cook gently in the spices and oil until coated in the mixture and beginning to brown – this should take only about 5–8 minutes. Mix in the chilli and garlic and cook for a further 2 minutes. Remove from the heat and stir in the spring onions, lemon juice and chopped coriander. Set aside and allow to cool.

Divide the dough into 20 balls. Flatten each ball and roll out on a floured surface to make a circle approximately 10cm/4in across. Spoon a heaped tablespoon of the potato mixture into the centre of each circle, then brush the edge with a little water. Fold over the pastry to form a semi-circle and seal by pressing the edges together. Continue in this way until you have made 20 pasties, covering the finished pasties with a damp cloth or cling film as you make the rest.

Heat about 9cm/4in of oil in a wok or heavy-based saucepan over a medium heat. To test the temperature, drop a little of the pastry into the oil – it should sizzle immediately. Fry the pasties in batches for 2–3 minutes until lightly browned. Remove with a slotted spoon and drain on kitchen paper. Serve warm with a mango chutney and coriander dipping sauce.

curried football pie

When I travelled up to Grimsby Town Football Club to taste their famous pies, it became clear that a hand-held pie was intrinsic to the ritual of the game. At half-time, a pie and a cup of Bovril were not only a tasty affair but, more importantly, a warming and comforting pep-up on a freezing day and something to get you through the second half. You supporters are a hardy bunch, so with you in mind I have developed the perfect recipe for wintry days with a hint of spice for added heat. These pies are equally delicious served at home with an ice-cold beer.

makes 4 pies

for the pastry
400g/13oz shortcrust pastry (see page 15) · milk, to glaze

for the filling
2 tbsp butter · 2 large onions, finely chopped · 2 cloves garlic, crushed · 2cm/1in piece ginger, grated · 3 tbsp hot Madras curry paste · 8 skinless chicken thigh fillets, about 900g/1³/₄lb in total weight, cut into cubes · 250ml/8fl oz chicken stock · 200ml/7fl oz carton coconut cream
1 green chilli, deseeded and finely chopped · salt and ground black pepper

Heat the butter in a large pan, add the onions and cook for about 5 minutes until softened. Add the garlic, ginger and curry paste and cook for 1 minute.

Add the chicken to the hot spiced butter and coat well. Pour over the chicken stock and the coconut cream and simmer for 20–25 minutes until the sauce has thickened. Remove from the heat and leave to cool.

Preheat the oven to 200°C/400°F/Gas 6.

Roll out half of the pastry and use it to line 4 individual 7 x 5cm/3 x 2in pie dishes, 3.5cm/1¹/₂in deep. Spoon the chicken curry into each dish and sprinkle over a little green chilli. Roll out the remaining pastry and cut out 4 lids. Place a lid on top of each pie and press the edges together to seal. Brush the tops with a little milk to glaze and bake for 30 minutes until golden. Remove from the tins and serve.

the football pie

The tradition of hot pies at football and rugby matches has become one of the essential elements of watching a game. It's hard to pin-point when this union began, but pies were the original British fast food long before the advent of burgers and fried chicken.

As the football season runs through the coldest period of the year, a hot hand-held pie really is the only logical food to keep hunger and the elements at bay. It's a match-day tradition that's been around for years and a hot pie is definitely something that supporters are very passionate about.

While the hand-held pies being sold at kiosks and vans all over the country may not in the past have been of the highest quality, they were certainly enjoyed in vast quantities. Today, however, the pies are finding themselves competing in a league of their own. Not only do the supporters have a favourite football ground, but they have favourite pie vendors and the all-round experience of the game is determined by the quality of the pies. In fact the ultimate football pie now has very stringent criteria. It must have

just the right ratio of pastry to filling and must be the right size to be hand-held or to serve in a small tray with peas and gravy. Supporters are now so discerning that a pie league table has been set up where you can vote for your favourite pies across the country and messages are posted from devoted pie fans.

The association of pies and sport has spread far and wide. In the 19th century, many English sports were exported to Australia and with them the practice of eating and enjoying pies. Indeed the Australians are now reputed to be the world's largest consumer of meat pies *per capita*, with each person eating, on average, over 12 meat pies and a further 17 combined pastries, sausage rolls and party pies every year.

As they are a staple of football fans the world over, it's perhaps no surprise that today pies have their own chant and any player who looks like they've been overindulging is sure to be regaled with a rousing 'Who ate all the pies?'.

cornish pasties

This traditional snack from Cornwall used to be marked with the initials of the person for whom it was intended, whether it be a miner, fisherman or farmer. The fillings varied somewhat – no doubt depending on what was available at the time and the wealth of the household. They were usually made with meat and potatoes, although sometimes other vegetables were added. They still are one of the most popular hand-held pies and when made well are a delicious combination of simple succulent filling and the lightest pastry ever. Place the lard and butter in the freezer for about 20 minutes before you start to make the pasties as this will give you a really crisp pastry.

makes 4 large pasties

for the pastry
450g/14¹/₂oz strong plain flour · pinch salt · 100g/3¹/₂oz lard, chilled in the freezer
100g/3¹/₂oz butter, chilled in the freezer · beaten egg, to glaze

for the filling
250g/8oz beef skirt, chopped into rough cubes about 5mm/¹/₄in square · 225g/8oz potatoes,
peeled and diced into 5mm/¹/₄in cubes · 225g/8oz swede, peeled and diced into 5mm/¹/₄in cubes
1 onion, finely chopped · 1 tbsp vegetable oil · salt and ground black pepper

For the pastry, sift the flour and salt into a bowl, then grate in the lard and butter straight from the
freezer. Gently mix through the flour and stir in enough cold water to bring the mixture together to
make a firm dough. Knead briefly and form into a smooth ball. Wrap in cling film and chill in the fridge
for 20 minutes.

Preheat the oven to 180°C/350°F/Gas 4.

For the filling, combine the beef with the potatoes, swede,
onion, vegetable oil, a little salt and black pepper.

Cut the pastry into 4 even-sized pieces. Roll out each
piece until it is large enough to cut out a 20cm/8in circle.
Divide the beef and vegetable mixture between the
4 pastry circles, piling it along the middle of the pastry.
Brush the rim of the pastry with beaten egg. Bring up
the pastry from either side to meet in the middle and
pinch together to make a scalloped edge down the
centre. Make 2 slits with a sharp knife so that steam
can escape through the pastry during cooking.

Place on a baking sheet and brush with beaten egg. Bake for 35–40 minutes until the pastry is golden.
The pasties are delicious served hot, straight from the oven, and I must confess to eating
them with a little HP brown sauce.

sausage rolls

It couldn't be simpler to make delicious sausage rolls – there is a multitude of good sausages around as well as great ready-made puff pastry. These are made using Cumberland sausages spruced up with onion, herbs and a little Parmesan cheese for flavour. I love no-nonsense, substantial sausage rolls – big and juicy ones that you can sink your teeth into – but for a more refined affair you can make little bite-sized ones to serve with drinks.

makes 8 large or 16 small rolls

for the pastry
500g/1lb ready-made puff pastry · beaten egg, to glaze

for the filling
8 large Cumberland sausages, skins removed · 1 small onion, finely chopped
3–4 sage leaves, finely chopped · 3 tbsp chopped flat-leaf parsley · 3 tbsp grated Parmesan cheese
salt and ground black pepper

Preheat the oven to 200°C/400°F/Gas 6.

To make the filling, mix the sausage meat in a bowl with the onion, sage, parsley and Parmesan. It's easiest to mulch it all together with your hands. Season with salt and ground black pepper.

Now assemble the first batch of sausage rolls. Cut the pastry in half and roll out one piece to make a long oblong shape, 40 x 17cm/16 x 6½in and 3mm/⅛in thick. Form half the filling into a long log-shape which will run the whole length of the pastry. Place the sausage log 5mm/¼in in from the edge of the pastry. Egg-wash the entire length of the pastry strip, then fold the pastry over the log and press down well to seal the edges, either crimping them with your fingers or pressing down with a fork.

Cut the pastry-covered log into 4 individual rolls if you want large ones, or 8 bite-sized rolls. Brush with egg to glaze and then place on a baking tray lined with greased baking parchment, leaving plenty of space in between each one. Place the tray in the oven for 35–40 minutes and bake until the rolls are golden, risen and flaky. Remove from the oven and allow to cool slightly on a wire rack.

While the sausage rolls are baking, prepare a second batch using the remaining pastry and filling. Serve the rolls while still warm.

Home-made sausage rolls straight from the oven have got to be the best hand–held pies ever – well my dog and I think so anyway.

smoked salmon, prawn and herb pies

Crammed with smoked salmon, prawns and herbs, these pies are a luxurious treat. Short-cut flaky pastry provides the perfect contrast to the tasty filling, giving a crisp, light and buttery coating. These pies are great served hot or cold with a crisp green salad, or wrap them up and take them to the seaside for a picnic. Fish eaten by the sea always tastes fantastic.

makes 6 pies

for the pastry
450g/14^1/$_2$oz short-cut flaky pastry (see page 19) · beaten egg, to glaze

for the filling
200g/7oz smoked salmon, chopped · 250g/8oz small raw prawns · 25g/1oz Parmesan cheese, grated · 2 tbsp chopped fresh dill · 1 clove garlic, finely chopped · 150g/5oz mascarpone cheese grated zest 1 lemon · ground black pepper

Preheat the oven to 200°C/400°F/Gas 6.

On a floured surface, roll out the pastry to form a large sheet 3mm/^{1}/$_8$in thick and cut out 6 circles of 12cm/5in diameter and 6 circles of 15cm/6in diameter.

Mix together the smoked salmon, prawns, Parmesan, chopped dill, garlic, mascarpone, lemon zest and plenty of ground black pepper.

Dollop 2–3 tablespoons of the mixture in the centre of each of the smaller circles. Brush the edges of the circles with a little egg. Position the larger circles on top and press the pastry edges together to seal.

Use a sharp knife to create a small hole in the centre of each and then transfer to a baking sheet. Brush the pies with a little beaten egg and bake for about 20 minutes until golden and crisp.

Serve hot or cold.

fennel and gruyère puffs

These little pies are really simple to make using good-quality, ready-made puff pastry. Don't worry if they look like strange UFOs when they come out of the oven – they will still taste delicious and are great served warm as appetisers with drinks.

makes 12 puffs

for the pastry
375g/12oz ready-rolled puff pastry · beaten egg, to glaze

for the filling
2 tbsp olive oil · 1 small onion, finely chopped · 1 small fennel bulb, finely chopped
1 tsp fennel seeds · 25g/1oz butter · 75g/3oz Gruyère cheese, grated
salt and ground black pepper

For the filling, heat the oil and butter in a large frying pan and add the onion, fennel and fennel seeds and fry very gently for about 15 minutes until softened, then stir through the grated cheese. Remove from the heat and allow to cool slightly.

Unroll the pastry and cut out 12 rounds of 5cm/2in diameter for the lids and 12 rounds of 4cm/1¹/₂in diameter for the bases. Place the smaller pastry bases on a large baking sheet and brush the edges with beaten egg.

Spoon the cooled fennel mixture on to the pastry bases, leaving a 1cm/¹/₂in margin. Position the pastry lids on top and use a fork to press the pastry edges together to seal. Chill in the fridge for 30 minutes.

Preheat the oven to 220°C/425°F/Gas 7.

Brush the top of the puffs with beaten egg and bake for 20 minutes until golden brown and puffed up. Serve warm.

lamb en croûtes

These little parcels comprise tasty layers of spinach, mushrooms and tender lamb, all wrapped in rich shortcrust pastry which seals in the juices and keeps everything deliciously moist.

makes 4 *en croûtes*

for the pastry
300g/10oz rich shortcrust pastry (see page 16) · beaten egg, to glaze

for the filling
4 tbsp olive oil · 4 lamb fillets, each weighing 150g/5oz · large knob butter
125g/4oz chestnut mushrooms, finely chopped · 1 clove garlic, finely chopped
4 sun-dried tomatoes, finely chopped · 2 canned anchovy fillets, finely chopped
small bunch fresh mint finely chopped · 200g/7oz large spinach leaves · 3 tbsp Marsala
1 tbsp redcurrant jelly · 300ml/¹/₂ pint lamb stock · salt and ground black pepper

Preheat the oven to 200°C/400°F/Gas 6.

For the filling, heat half the oil in a large frying pan and seal the lamb until browned. Remove from the pan and set aside. In the same pan heat the remaining oil with the butter until the butter is foaming. Stir in the mushrooms and cook for about 15 minutes until browned and tender. Stir in the garlic, sun-dried tomatoes and anchovies and season to taste. Cook for 5 minutes until the mixture has a soft, paste-like consistency. Remove from the heat, stir in the chopped mint and set aside.

Wash the spinach leaves and place in a saucepan with just the water that clings to them. Cook gently, being careful not to break the leaves, until just wilted. Drain well and leave to cool. Spread the mushroom paste over each piece of lamb and carefully wrap the spinach leaves around the paste.

Roll out the pastry on a lightly floured surface until about 3mm/¹/₈in thick. Cut into 4 and wrap each piece around a piece of lamb. Place the parcels, sealed side down, on a baking tray and brush with beaten egg. Bake for 25–30 minutes until the pastry is crispy and golden.

Meanwhile, reheat the pan used for the lamb and pour in the Marsala. Deglaze the pan, scraping up any bits left on the bottom, then stir in the redcurrant jelly. Add the stock and simmer gently until the mixture is syrupy and has reduced by about half. Serve the *en croûtes* with the Marsala gravy.

asparagus turnovers

These are sort of half-pie and half-tart – a delicious, creamy ham and cheese filling with asparagus spears wrapped in puff pastry. Very simple and very tasty, they are perfect for a quick supper *(illustrated on preceding pages)*.

makes 6 turnovers

for the pastry
500g/1lb ready-made puff pastry

for the filling
100g/3^{1}/2oz cream cheese · grated zest and juice ^{1}/2 lemon · 15g/^{1}/2oz fresh chives, chopped
25g/1oz Parmesan cheese, grated · 6 thin slices cooked smoked ham · 600g/1^{1}/4lb asparagus
spears, trimmed · 1 tbsp olive oil · salt and ground black pepper

Preheat the oven to 200°C/400°F/Gas 6.

Roll out the pastry on a lightly floured surface to form a sheet 3mm/^{1}/8in thick. Now cut it into 6 even-sized squares.

Place the cream cheese, lemon zest and juice, chives and most of the Parmesan in a bowl and mix together well. Season with a little salt and ground black pepper. Divide the mixture between the 6 pastry squares, spreading it out a little, then lay a slice of cooked ham on the cheese. Place a few asparagus spears diagonally on top of the ham. Now fold the bottom corner of each pastry square over the base of the spears, leaving the tips exposed. Brush the edges of the pastry with a little water. Fold over each side of the pastry to form a pouch, pressing down gently to seal.

Brush the top of the pastry and asparagus tips with the oil and sprinkle with the remaining Parmesan. Bake for 20 minutes until the pastry is golden and puffed and the asparagus spears are tender. Serve immediately.

goat's cheese, roasted garlic and sweet potato parcels

Oozing goat's cheese wrapped in flaky pastry with the sweetness of roasted garlic and sweet potatoes – what a joy! These parcels make a divine supper served with a salad of peppery chicory and rocket leaves.·

makes 4 parcels

for the pastry
375g/12oz ready-rolled puff pastry · beaten egg, to glaze

for the filling
1 tbsp olive oil · 2 sweet potatoes, weighing about 500g/1lb, peeled and thinly sliced
3 sprigs fresh thyme · 8 cloves garlic, skins left on · 2 soft barrel-shaped goat's cheeses
salt and ground black pepper

Preheat the oven to 200°C/400°F/Gas 6.

Toss the olive oil, sweet potatoes, most of the thyme and the garlic in a large roasting tin. Add a little salt and plenty of ground black pepper and roast on a high shelf in the oven for about 15 minutes until the sweet potatoes are tender and golden and the garlic is soft and paste-like when squeezed. Remove from the roasting tin and leave to cool.

Unroll the pastry and cut it into 4 squares of about 18cm/7in.

Squeeze the roasted garlic out of its skin and spread over the base of each pastry square, using about 2 cloves of garlic per square. Use half of the sweet potato slices to cover the garlic, and add a little more thyme. Cut each goat's cheese in half and arrange on top of the sweet potatoes. Arrange the remaining sweet potato slices on top.

Fold the corners of each pastry square into the centre to make an envelope and cover the filling. Crimp the edges to seal. Place the parcels on a baking tray, brush with beaten egg and bake for 20 minutes until the pastry is golden and puffed and the cheese has softened. Eat while the cheese is still warm.

empanadillas

These small, crescent-shaped pasties are traditionally served as tapas with drinks but are equally good eaten at any time. The filling reflects both North African and Catalan influences with the use of cumin, paprika and the sweet contrast of raisins. The dough has a soft, pliable texture, making it easy to shape and form the little pasties.

makes 20 empanadillas

for the pastry
350g/11¹/₂oz plain flour · ¹/₄ tsp salt · 175g/6oz butter, melted
1 egg, beaten · 100ml/3¹/₂fl oz warm water · milk, to glaze

for the filling
1 tbsp vegetable oil · 1 onion, finely chopped
350g/11¹/₂oz minced beef . 1 red pepper, finely chopped
2 cloves garlic, finely chopped · 1 tbsp tomato purée . 1 tsp chilli flakes · 1 tsp cumin seeds
1 tsp smoked paprika · 25g/1oz raisins · salt and ground black pepper

To make the pastry, sift the flour and salt into a large bowl. Stir in the butter and egg and then gradually work in enough warm water to make a firm dough. Knead for 5–10 minutes until the dough is smooth. Leave to rest, covered in cling film, for 15 minutes while you prepare the filling.

For the filling, heat the oil in a large pan and cook the onion for a few minutes until it begins to soften. Stir in the minced beef and cook until browned. Add the red pepper, garlic, tomato purée, chilli flakes, cumin seeds, paprika and raisins and season well with salt and plenty of ground black pepper. Add a few tablespoons of water at this stage if the mixture looks too dry. Simmer for 5 minutes and then remove from the heat and leave to cool.

Preheat the oven to 200°C/400°F/Gas 6.

Roll out the pastry to a thickness of about 3mm/¹/₈in. Use a saucer as a template to cut out 24 circles measuring about 12cm/5in in diameter. Divide the filling between the dough circles and moisten the edges with a little water. Fold over the dough to enclose the filling and press along the edges to seal. Pinch the sealed edges and twist over to create a rope effect, or simply press a fork along the edges. Glaze with a little milk and bake for 10–15 minutes until golden. Serve warm.

scallop, crab and cayenne pies

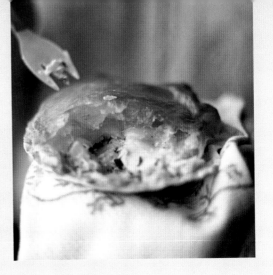

It really makes sense to use the scallop shells as pie dishes for these tasty individual pies. Just give them a good scrub once you've removed the scallops. Alternatively, ask your fishmonger to keep some shells aside for you, as not all sell scallops in the shell.

makes 4 pies

for the pastry
375g/12oz ready-rolled puff pastry · milk, to glaze

for the filling
20g/³/4oz butter · 2 shallots, finely chopped · 6 thin rashers pancetta, finely chopped
8 large scallops, including the coral · 150g/5oz white crab meat · pinch cayenne
grated zest ¹/2 lemon · 2 tbsp finely chopped flat-leaf parsley · 3 tbsp fromage frais
salt and ground black pepper

Preheat the oven to 200°C/400°F/Gas 6.

Heat the butter in a small frying pan and gently cook the shallots for a few minutes. Add the pancetta and cook for a further 3 minutes. Slice each scallop horizontally into 3 rounds and halve the coral. Place the scallops, corals and crab meat in a bowl and stir in the shallots and pancetta with the cayenne, lemon zest and parsley. Stir through the fromage frais and season with salt and black pepper.

Divide the mixture between 4 cleaned and dried scallop shells and place on a baking tray.

Roll out the pastry to a thickness of 3mm/¹/8in and cut out 4 rounds of pastry about 1cm/¹/2in larger than the scallop shells. Lay each piece of pastry loosely over the top of each shell so that it covers the filling, press it down on to the shell edge to shape, then cut away any excess pastry. Brush with a little milk and bake for 15 minutes until the pastry is puffed and golden. Serve immediately.

scotch pies

Large numbers of Scotch pies are sold every day in Scotland – many at half-time during football matches. They are the ultimate hot fast food, easily eaten in the hand or served with gravy, peas or beans. Traditionally they're made using straight-sided moulds 8cm/3½in in diameter and about 4cm/1½in deep, but you could easily use an upturned jam jar. The pastry lid is pressed on top of the pie slightly lower than the rim to create a space for the gravy.

Each butcher or baker has their own recipe with an individual mixture of spices and secret ingredients, but Scotch pies always contain lamb or mutton and a grinding of mace or nutmeg. Try to buy good-quality lean mince as it really does make a difference to the finished pie.

If you don't want to bake all your pies at once, you can freeze them uncooked and simply defrost and bake when desired (*illustrated on preceding pages*).

makes 8 pies

for the pastry
450g/14½oz hot-water crust pastry (see page 21) · beaten egg, to glaze

for the filling
1 tsp vegetable oil · 450g/14½oz lean minced lamb · 1 tsp Worcestershire sauce
1 small onion, finely chopped · ¼ tsp ground nutmeg · 4 tbsp lamb stock
salt and ground black pepper

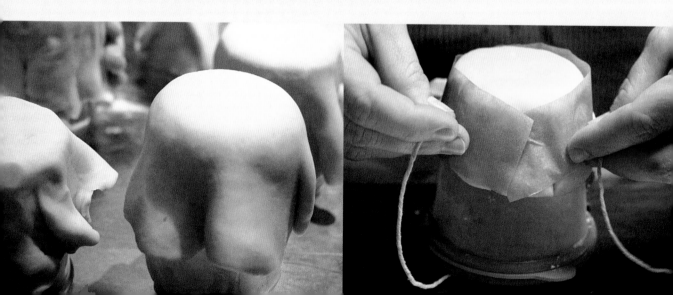

Preheat the oven to 180°C/350°F/Gas 4.

Use the oil to lightly grease the outer sides and bottoms of 8 jam jars measuring 8cm/3¹/₂in in diameter (if you don't have 8 jars just make the pastry cases in 2 batches). Divide the pastry into 2 pieces. Place 1 in the fridge to make the lids and use the other to form 8 balls. On a lightly floured surface, roll out the balls to an even thickness of about 5mm/¹/₄in, making pastry rounds large enough to fit the upturned jam jar bottoms and to come about 6cm/2¹/₂in down the sides of the jars. Press each round on to the bottom of a jar and up against the sides, then set aside to cool.

Cut 8 strips of greaseproof paper the same depth as the pastry cases and long enough to wrap around the jars. Wrap each strip of paper around a case and secure with string. Place the finished pie shells in the fridge to firm up for about 30 minutes.

Meanwhile, mix all of the filling ingredients together, seasoning well with salt and ground black pepper.

Gently slide the pastry cases off the jars and place them on a baking sheet. Divide the meat mixture between the pastry cases, pressing it down well.

Roll out the remaining pastry to make 8 lids for the pies. Dampen the edges of the pies and place a lid on each, pressing them down lower than the rim. Crimp the edges with your fingers to seal.

Brush with beaten egg to glaze and cut a hole in the centre, to allow steam to escape. Bake for 45 minutes, or until lightly golden, then serve hot with gravy (see page 185) poured on top and into the steam hole.

Barney's beef and stilton corner-shop pies

This is my great friend Barney's genius recipe for the most delicious and simple pies you'll ever taste. The corner-shop reference is where the genius bit comes in. No need for weighing or any tricky techniques, the pastry for these pies is pure simplicity and uses ready-weighed ingredients that are all available at your local corner shop!

This recipe makes enough filling for 8 individual pies or, like me, you can eat half the meat as a stew on the day you cook it and freeze or chill the other half as a pie filling. The filling is basically beef braised in red wine, given an extra kick by a splash of balsamic vinegar and a sprinkling of chilli. The Stilton cheese, which is crumbled in just before the lids go on, gives the pies their sublime flavour.

makes 8 pies

for the pastry
500g/1lb bag plain flour · 250g/8oz pack butter, diced · 1 egg, beaten, plus 1 extra to glaze
70–100ml/3–3¹/₂fl oz water · salt and ground black pepper

for the filling
2 tbsp sunflower oil · 1kg/2lb braising beef, cut into very large chunks
4 carrots, peeled and cut into very large chunks · 1 large onion, roughly chopped · 1 clove garlic
small pinch chilli flakes · 4 tbsp flour · big splash balsamic vinegar · 1 bottle full-bodied red wine
1 bouquet garni (tie a bunch of parsley stalks, a branch of bay leaves and a bunch of thyme together
with string · 150g/5oz Stilton cheese, crumbled

To make the pastry, tip the flour, butter, a pinch of salt and some pepper into a food processor
and pulse until the mixture has the texture of breadcrumbs. Pour in the egg and water and pulse
again until the pastry comes together to form a ball. Wrap and chill in the fridge for at least
30 minutes before using.

Preheat the oven to 160°C/325°F/Gas 3.

Heat the oil in a large flameproof casserole dish until smoking, add half the beef and leave it to brown
for about 5 minutes (don't be tempted to prod it, stir it, or lift it up). Stir once and continue to brown
the meat, then remove it to a plate with a slotted spoon and repeat with the second batch of beef.

Once the second batch of beef has been removed, add the carrots, onion, garlic and chilli to the pan
and cook for 8–10 minutes until the vegetables are starting to soften. Stir in the flour and cook for
2 minutes until the flour begins to brown. Add a splash of balsamic vinegar and allow the mixture to
simmer for 2 minutes, then stir in the red wine. Tip the beef and any juices back into the pan and season
generously with salt and a little pepper. Bring to the boil, add the bouquet garni, cover and place in the
oven for about 2 hours until the meat is meltingly tender. Remove from the oven and leave to cool.

Turn the oven up to 220°C/425°F/Gas 7 and heat a baking tray while you roll out the pastry.
Roll out the pastry on a floured surface to 3mm/1/8in thick and cut out pieces to fit 8 individual pie
tins (or foil trays).

Spoon the cooled filling into the pastry cases and sprinkle on the Stilton. Cut out the remaining pastry
to make lids for the pies. Wet the pastry edges with a little water and place the lids on top. Seal the
edges by pressing together, then trim away any excess pastry. Brush the tops with beaten egg to glaze.

Place the pies on the hot tray and bake for 10 minutes, then lower the oven temperature to 180°C/
350°F/Gas 4 and cook for 30 minutes until the tops are golden. Remove from the oven and leave to
rest for 10 minutes. The pies should now turn out of their tins easily and the bottoms should be crisp.

noblepie

These are not everyday pies, but something to create for a special occasion. They are 'noble' because of the time and effort needed to create all the curves, flutings, cornices, roses, diamonds, circles and leaves used for decoration. I guarantee a real sense of achievement when you remove the pie from its tin and present it to be sliced.

Steeped in history, these pies originate from the days when pastry was used simply as a container to protect and preserve the meat inside and was then discarded rather than eaten (though of course today we wouldn't dream of throwing it away). As a result, these pies use hot-water crust pastry (see page 21), which defies all the normal rules for pastry making and gives a pastry of considerable strength which is sturdy enough to act as a container.

Hot-water crust is a filling pastry because the pie walls must have thickness for strength and also to withstand the long cooking time needed to heat the dense filling inside. The pastry absorbs the rich meat juices and fat during cooking, but remains crisp outside.

Noble pies are often called 'raised' pies because they are raised or shaped by hand and were traditionally prepared by pressing the dough on to the outside of a wooden mould. If you don't have a special tin or mould, you can form your pie around a jam jar or in a cake tin with a removable base. Think of the dough as a piece of clay – it is warm and malleable and you can easily shape it into the mould or tin, repairing any cracks and holes.

The filling of a raised pie shrinks during cooking and the gap is filled with a savoury jelly – hot stock which sets when cold. The jelly adds flavour and also keeps the meat moist. It's very simple to make, but does mean planning a couple of days ahead. For a good stock, use the bones from the meat you are using and simmer for a few hours with pig's trotters, vegetables and herbs. The stock will keep in the fridge for a few days until you need it.

raised game pie

This pie looks rather spectacular when cooked in a traditional pie tin. You can pick up tins of this sort from vintage cookware shops and even hunt them out on the web. They are rather expensive to buy new and an investment only if you know you are going to use them regularly. However, this pie is equally wonderful made in a loose-bottomed spring-form cake tin.

You can vary the filling depending on what you want to use and what is around at the time: venison, pheasant and wild rabbit are all delicious. My butcher is a game specialist and so has game mix ready prepared, boned and chopped, which makes life very easy.

serves 8

for the pastry
500g/1lb hot-water crust pastry (see page 21) to fill a 20cm/8in deep pie mould
beaten egg, to glaze

for the filling
25g/1oz butter · 1 onion, finely chopped · 2 cloves garlic, finely chopped
900g/1³/4lb mixed boneless game meat, such as pheasant, pigeon breast, venison or rabbit
cut into 1cm/¹/2in pieces · 2 tbsp brandy · 450g/14¹/2oz pork loin, minced
pinch ground cinnamon · pinch ground ginger · 4 tbsp chopped mixed herbs, such as parsley
and thyme · 225g/8oz thin rashers smoked bacon · salt and ground black pepper

for the jellied stock
600ml/1 pint jellied stock (see Melton Mowbray Pie, page 127), made using reserved bones
from the game

Heat the butter in a large frying pan, add the onion and garlic and cook gently until softened. Remove from the heat and transfer to a large bowl. Stir in the game meat, brandy, pork, cinnamon, ginger and herbs and season well to taste. Set aside.

Preheat the oven to 200°C/400°F/Gas 6. Place a heavy-duty baking tray in the oven.

Cut off one-third of the pastry and set this aside for the lid. Roll out the larger piece to about 12cm/5in larger than the base of your raised pie mould or tin (you can use a 20cm/8in loose-bottomed cake tin) and use it to line the base and sides, leaving a little excess pastry overhanging the sides. Make sure there are no cracks or holes and that the pastry is evenly distributed around the tin. Roll out the remaining pastry to fit the top of the pie and set aside.

Arrange the rashers of bacon in the base of the pastry case, so that they come up the sides. Pile the game mixture in the centre and mound in the middle to support the lid. Brush the overhanging pastry edges with a little beaten egg and then place the pastry lid on top. Pinch and crimp the edges of the case and lid to seal and trim away any excess pastry. Brush the top with egg to glaze. Use the excess pastry to make leaves to decorate the top. Brush with beaten egg and make a steam hole in the middle of the lid. Place the pie on the hot baking tray and bake for 30 minutes, then reduce the oven temperature to 160°C/325°F/Gas 3 and bake for a further 2 hours. Cover the lid with a sheet of tin foil if the top starts to brown too quickly.

Warm the jellied stock until melted and then pour in through the steam hole while the pie is still warm. Leave to cool completely before removing the pie from the tin and cutting into slices to serve.

raised fish pie

As fish requires much less cooking than meat, you won't need hot-water crust pastry for this pie. A rich shortcrust pastry, made with a mixture of butter and lard, makes a great container for the delicate filling. Serve it cold, cut into wedges, with a creamy lemon and herb mayonnaise.

makes a 18cm/7in pie

for the pastry
300g/10oz rich shortcrust pastry (see page 16) · milk, to glaze

for the filling
450g/14¹/₂oz salmon fillet · 300ml/¹/₂ pint fish stock · 225g/8oz smoked salmon · 1 egg, beaten
2 tbsp double cream · juice and grated zest 1 lemon · small bunch flat-leaf parsley, finely chopped
ground black pepper

Preheat the oven to 200°C/400°F/Gas 6. Place a heavy-duty baking tray in the oven.

Roll out two-thirds of the pastry to make a circle large enough to line the base and sides of an 18cm/7in loose-bottomed cake tin, leaving a 2cm/³/₄in overhang of excess pastry. Roll out the remaining pastry to make a lid. Chill in the fridge until needed.

Place the salmon in a deep frying pan, pour over the fish stock and bring to a simmer. Poach for 4–5 minutes until the fish flakes easily. Strain well, reserving 4 tablespoons of stock to pour into the pie after baking. Flake the fish into pieces.

Place the smoked salmon in a food processor and whiz with the egg, cream, lemon juice and zest and parsley. Season with plenty of ground black pepper.

Spread the smoked salmon paste on to the base and sides of your pastry case and then pile the flaked salmon fillet into the centre of the tin.

Brush the edges of the pastry with a little milk and then place the lid on top and pinch and crimp the edges of the case and lid to seal, trimming away any excess pastry. Brush the top of the pie with the remaining milk and bake for 35 minutes until golden. Pour the reserved stock into the pie through the steam hole, before allowing the pie to cool.

melton mowbray pork pie

Making a pork pie is not difficult – it just takes time rather than any special skill. It really is worth the effort, as it's immensely satisfying to create something so grand and delicious.

Get your butcher to remove the bones from the pork shoulder so you can keep them for the jellied stock and ask for a pig's trotter too, as this really does give the best flavour. You can recognise a true hand-raised Melton Mowbray pie from the way the sides are slightly bowed, where the pie has been baked and then collapsed a little. However, there's a real skill to raising a pie by hand, and to make life easier I use a 20cm/8in loose-bottomed cake tin.

If you're making individual pies, simply shape the pastry for each pie over a jam jar (as for the Scotch Pies, page 110), wrap it with a strip of greaseproof paper and tie a piece of string around the middle before removing the case.

makes 1 x 20cm/8in pie or 6 individual 10cm/4in pies

for the pastry
500g/1lb hot-water crust pastry (see page 21) · beaten egg, to glaze

for the jellied stock
bones from the pork plus 1 pig's trotter · 1 large carrot · 1 onion
1 bouquet garni of celery, bay leaf, thyme and parsley · salt · 12 black peppercorns

for the filling
900g/13¾lb boned pork shoulder · 250g/8oz thick rashers bacon · 2 tbsp chopped fresh sage
pinch each ground nutmeg, cinnamon and allspice · 1 tsp anchovy essence, or to taste

First make the jelly. Put all the ingredients in a large saucepan and cover with 1.5 litres/2½ pints of water. Bring to the boil, then put on the lid and cook gently for 2 hours. Strain the stock through a sieve, return to the saucepan and boil rapidly until the liquid has reduced to about 600ml/1pint. Season with a little salt and leave to cool. This will keep in the fridge for up to 4 days.

For the filling, chop the pork and bacon into 1cm/½in pieces. Place half the pork and bacon into a food processor and process, using the pulse button, until coarsely chopped. Transfer to a bowl with the rest of the chopped pork and bacon and mix together with the sage, spices and anchovy essence.

Cut off one-third of the pastry and set aside for the lid. Roll out the larger piece to a circle about 26cm/10½in, so that it's large enough to line the base and sides of a 20cm/8in loose-bottomed spring-form cake tin with some pastry overhanging the sides (if you're making individual pies, follow the method for Scotch Pies on page 110). Roll out the remaining pastry to fit the top of the pie.

Preheat the oven to 200°C/400°F/Gas 6.

Pack the filling into the pastry case, mounding it up slightly to support the lid. Moisten the edges of the pastry with beaten egg, lay the lid on top and pinch and crimp the edges of the case and lid to seal. Trim away any excess pastry, brush with beaten egg and create a hole in the centre.

Bake for 30 minutes, then lower the temperature to 160°C/325°F/Gas 3 and bake for 60 minutes. (If you're making individual pies, bake for 20 minutes at 200°C/400°F/Gas 6, then for 50 minutes at 160°C/325°F/ Gas 3.) Remove the pie from the oven and unclip the outer tin. Brush the pastry with the remaining beaten egg and return to the oven for a further 30 minutes until golden brown.

Allow the pie to cool slightly then heat the jellied stock in a saucepan and slowly pour it into the warm pie, ideally using a funnel. The stock needs to be hot so that it sinks into the filling. Don't hurry this process or you will flood the outer crust of the pie.

Leave the pie to go completely cold overnight before serving it cut into wedges.

veal and ham raised pie

We are probably more familiar with this pie in its mass-produced form, when it is called gala pie. You will know it as the one with the egg that runs through the centre. How do they make it so that everyone gets a slice of egg?! That's a mystery we will never know the answer to.

There are many historical recipes for this pie and lots of regional variations. Traditionally it contains veal and cooked ham – a far cry from the manufactured gala pie, which is made with pork and ham. This version has a wonderful light and flavoursome filling and is certainly worth the time and effort for a special occasion. I love to eat it with pickles, mustard, radish, a tasty, sharp hard cheese and a glass of dry cider – yum *(illustrated on preceding pages)*.

serves 8

for the pastry
500g/1lb hot-water crust pastry (see page 21) · beaten egg, to glaze

for the filling
450g/14¹/₂oz stewing veal · 450g/14¹/₂oz cooked ham · 4 tbsp chopped flat-leaf parsley
grated zest and juice 1 lemon · 4 hard-boiled eggs, peeled · ground black pepper

for the jellied stock
200ml/7fl oz jellied stock (see Melton Mowbray Pork Pie, page 127), made in advance

Preheat the oven to 200°C/400°F/Gas 6. Place a heavy-duty baking tray in the oven.

Cut off one-third of the pastry and set this aside for the lid. Roll out the larger piece to an oblong shape large enough to line the base and sides of a 30 x 11cm/12 x 4¹/₂in loaf tin, with an overhang of about 2cm/³/₄in. Roll out the remaining pastry to fit the top of the pie and set aside.

Chop the veal and ham coarsely into 5mm/¹/₄in pieces. Place in a bowl and mix with the parsley, lemon zest and juice and plenty of ground black pepper (the ham will be quite salty, so you won't need to add salt).

Spread a layer of the meat mixture on top of the pastry and arrange the eggs lengthwise, one after the other, down the centre of the tin. Cover the eggs with the rest of the meat, pressing down gently.

Brush the edges of the pastry with a little beaten egg. Place the pastry lid on top of the filling and pinch and crimp the edges of the case and lid to seal, trimming away any excess pastry. Use the pastry trimmings to make decorative leaves. Brush the top of the pie with beaten egg and make a hole in the centre. Arrange the pastry leaves on top and brush with egg glaze.

Sit the pie on the baking tray and bake for 30 minutes, then reduce the oven temperature to 160°C/325°F/Gas 3 and cook for a further 1¹/₂ hours. If the lid starts to brown too quickly, cover the pie with a piece of tin foil.

Remove the pie from the oven and leave it to cool for 10 minutes.

Heat the jellied stock and pour it very slowly through a small funnel into the pie. Leave the pie to cool completely before serving it cut into slices.

Mrs King's pork pies

Brothers Paul, Ian and Neil Harland, who make Mrs King's Pork Pies at Cropwell Bishop in Nottinghamshire, really do know and love their product — authentic, hand-raised pork pies made with care. Ever since the first Melton Mowbray pie found popularity as a convenience food for Leicestershire huntsmen to carry in their saddlebags, the pies have been made with fresh rather than cured pork. This is one of the crucial distinctions between Melton Mowbray and other pork pies. Paul, who is a hands-on pie maker *extraordinaire*, insists on the best locally sourced pork and hand-chops all the fillings. Another distinguishing feature is the pie casing — it must be hot-water crust pastry and baked without any external support such as a tin or hoop. Watching Paul hand-raise the large pork pies, I'm sure that many other manufacturers don't

dedicate as much time and effort to their product — most mass-produced pies are now machine-made.

The hand-raised pies are shaped and filled, then baked on trays until browned and bubbling. A home-made jelly is then poured through the holes and allowed to cool and set. The attention and effort that goes into making

MELTON
MOWBRAY
PORK PIE

Min Meat 45%

£4.50

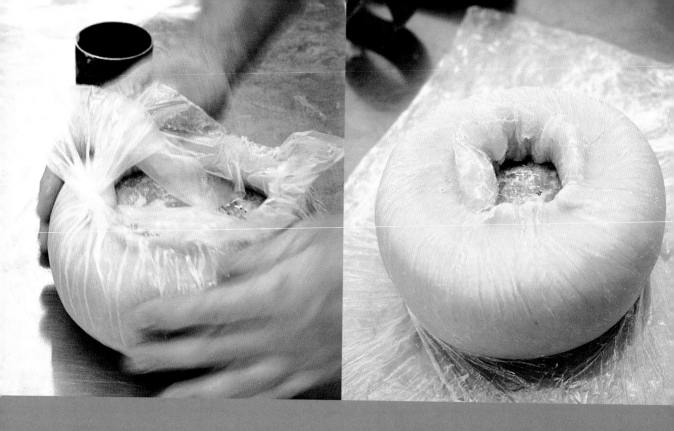

Authentic pork pies, hand-raised with love — you can expect crumbly pastry and firm, fresh-flavoured, succulent filling.

these pies is really shown in the finished result. They are delicious, crisp and tasty and I can't visit Borough Market in London, where they have a stall, without buying one.

Of the millions of pork pies manufactured in Britain each year only 3 million come from the Melton Mowbray area. Many companies elsewhere in the country add the name Melton Mowbray to their pies because it carries the weight of prestige and quality. Things, however, are about to change – an application has been made to the European Commission in Brussels for privileged status for authentic Melton Mowbray pies (as already exists for other famous British foods such as Stilton cheese, Newcastle Brown Ale, Whitstable oysters and Cornish clotted cream). It petitions that only pork pies produced in a clearly defined area in and around the Vale of Belvoir, made with the correct ingredients and by traditional methods, should be allowed to call themselves Melton Mowbray pies. Hopefully this

will end confusion as to the identity of a real Melton Mowbray pie, and when you buy one you can expect crumbly pastry and a firm, fresh-flavoured, succulent filling – just as delicious as they claim.

gooseberry raised pie

This is a fantastic old recipe which both tastes amazing and looks rather wonderful. It uses really simple ingredients and is a must when gooseberries are in season. Serve it in wedges with a large dollop of clotted cream.

makes a 15cm/6in pie

for the pastry
500g/1lb hot-water crust pastry (see page 21) · beaten egg, to glaze

for the filling
600g/1¼lb fresh gooseberries, topped and tailed · 200g/7oz jar apple jelly · 2 tbsp caster sugar

Preheat the oven to 200°C/400°F/Gas 6.

Cut off one-third of the pastry and set this aside for the lid. Roll out the larger piece to create a circle large enough to line the base and sides of a 15cm/6in loose-bottomed cake tin, with an overhang of about 2cm/³/₄in. Roll out the remaining pastry to fit the top of the pie.

Fill the pastry case with the gooseberries, mounding them up in the centre to support the lid, and brush the edges of the pastry case with a little beaten egg. Put on the pastry lid, pinching the edges of the case and lid to seal and trimming away any excess pastry. Make a small hole in the lid. Brush the top with a little beaten egg and sprinkle with caster sugar. Bake the pie for 30 minutes and then reduce the oven temperature to 180°C/350°F/Gas 4 and cook for a further 30 minutes.

Allow the pie to cool slightly. Place the apple jelly in a small saucepan and heat gently until it is melted and runny, then pour it through the hole in the lid using a small funnel. Allow the pie to cool completely before serving, cut into wedges.

raised venison pie with cranberry glaze

This pie offers a fine combination of flavours – rich port, gamey venison and tart cranberry. The glazed cranberry layer makes a great alternative to a pie crust, as well as being the perfect complement to the flavoursome filling.

makes an 18cm/7in square pie

for the pastry
450g/14¹/₂oz hot-water crust pastry (see page 21)

for the filling
900g/1³/₄lb venison neck, breast or shoulder, diced into 2cm/³/₄in cubes · 300ml/¹/₂ pint red wine or port · 25g/1oz butter · 2 shallots, finely chopped · 6 rashers smoked streaky bacon, finely chopped · 100g/3¹/₂oz calf's or lamb's liver, finely chopped · bunch flat-leaf parsley, finely chopped salt and ground black pepper · 4 tbsp redcurrant jelly · 250g/8oz fresh or frozen cranberries

for the jellied stock
200ml/7 fl oz jellied stock (see Melton Mowbray Pork Pie, page 127), made in advance

For the filling, place the venison in a large bowl, pour over the wine or port and season with a little salt and plenty of ground black pepper. Set aside.

Heat the butter in a large frying pan and gently cook the shallots for a few minutes until softened. Add the bacon and liver and cook for a few more minutes until browned all over. Remove from the heat and leave to cool.

Preheat the oven to 200°C/400°F/Gas 6. Place a heavy-duty baking tray in the oven.

Roll out the pastry to a circle large enough to line the base and sides of a 25cm/10in loose-bottomed cake tin with an overhang of about 2cm/³/₄in.

Add the shallot mixture and flat-leaf parsley to the venison, mix together, then spoon into the prepared pie case. Bake for 2 hours until the meat filling is completely cooked and tender. Allow to cool, then heat the jellied stock in a small saucepan and gently pour in as much stock as the pie will hold, reserving about 50ml/2fl oz for the glaze. Leave to cool and set.

Meanwhile heat the redcurrant jelly in a saucepan, tip in the cranberries and heat through until they begin to soften but still hold their shape. Spoon the cranberries over the top of the pie in a single layer, pour over the remaining jellied stock and allow to set.

sweetpie

Sweet pies are a truly wonderful thing – the only drawback is that you have to wait for them to cool before eating. The combination of a light, crispy pastry and sweet, juicy, seasonal fruits, creamy chocolate or dried fruits is the pure genius that has kept many of us happy for years.

From the humble apple pie served with a coating of creamy custard to traditional mince pies eaten with a dollop of brandy butter, these are recipes that have really stood the test of time and are still loved today.

The following recipes include a selection of familiar favourites as well as some equally fantastic new ideas. For the ultimate sweet-pie experience – traditional or otherwise – just serve a warm slice of pie on a plate with a liberal helping of custard or cream, or a few scoops of delicious ice cream. Yum!

chocolate-filled pear puddings

Tender pears filled with a chocolate and almond stuffing and wrapped in flaky pastry not only taste amazing but look pretty stunning too. This recipe works equally well with dessert apples.

serves 4

for the pastry
500g/1lb ready-made puff pastry · beaten egg, to glaze

for the filling
70g/2½oz plain chocolate · 3 tbsp double cream · 40g/1½oz ground almonds
4 tender ripe pears

Preheat the oven to 200°C/400°F/Gas 6.

Peel the pears but do not remove the stems. Using a vegetable corer, carefully core each pear from the bottom to within 2.5cm/1in of the top.

Place the chocolate in a small saucepan with the cream and heat very gently until the chocolate has melted. Remove from the heat and stir in the ground almonds. Set aside until cool enough to handle.

Fill the cavity of each pear with the chocolate mixture, pushing it up into the pear using a teaspoon or your thumb.

Roll out the pastry to create a large square sheet, about 3mm/⅛in thick and 40cm/16in square. Cut into 4 squares of 20cm/8in. Sit a filled pear in the centre of each square and wrap the pastry up and around the pear to cover. You may need to trim away any excess, but you can use this to make pastry leaves for decoration.

Paste any leaves on to the pears using a little water. Place the pears on a parchment-lined baking sheet and chill for about 30 minutes until ready to bake.

Lightly brush each pear with beaten egg to glaze and bake for 20–25 minutes until the pastry is puffed and lightly browned.

pear frangipane croustade

I love frangipane filling – that gooey, chewy texture – and it's especially delicious when combined with the flavour of pears. This recipe is based on the classic almond pie, pithiviers.

serves 8

for the pastry
500g/1lb ready-made puff pastry · beaten egg, to glaze · icing sugar, for dusting

for the filling
8 small ripe pears (tender Comice would be perfect) · grated zest and juice 1 lemon
125g/4oz butter, softened · 1 egg · 30ml/1fl oz dark rum or Cointreau · 75g/3oz caster sugar
200g/7oz ground almonds

Preheat the oven to 200°C/400°F/Gas 6.

Peel and core the pears and slice each one into 8 lengthways. Place the slices in a bowl and toss with the lemon zest and half the lemon juice. Beat the butter in a bowl until softened and then beat in the egg, rum or Cointreau, caster sugar, ground almonds and remaining lemon juice.

Cover a large baking tray with parchment paper. Roll out half of the pastry on a lightly floured surface until about 3mm/1/8in thick and cut out a 27cm/10½in circle using a plate as a guide. Lay the pastry on the baking tray. Spread the almond mixture on the pastry circle up to 2.5cm/1in from the edge. Top with the sliced pears.

Roll out the remaining pastry to a 28cm/11in round. Brush the edge of the pastry base with beaten egg, then carefully lay the pastry lid over the filling. Press the edges firmly to seal and scallop the edge of the pie decoratively, using a knife to make the indentations.

Brush the top with beaten egg to glaze and use a sharp knife to make faint lines radiating out from the centre to the edge in semi-circle patterns. Bake for about 30 minutes until well risen and golden. Dust the top generously with icing sugar and serve warm with cream or ice cream.

baby apple calvados pies

These luxurious apple pies are perfect served warm after dinner with a large dollop of sweetened mascarpone. Simply stir icing sugar into some mascarpone and, for extra luxury, add a splash of Calvados.

makes 12 pies

for the pastry
300g/10oz sweet shortcrust pastry (see page 15)

for the filling
25g/1oz butter · 8 tart apples, such as Granny Smith, peeled, cored and cut into 1cm/¹/₂in cubes
75g/3oz caster sugar, plus extra for dusting · ¹/₄ tsp ground cinnamon · grated zest ¹/₂ lemon
3 tbsp Calvados or brandy · 4 tbsp double cream

Melt the butter in a saucepan, then add the apples, sugar, cinnamon, lemon zest and Calvados. Toss together well in the pan and cook for 10 minutes until the apples have softened and you have a coarse purée. Leave to cool, then stir in the double cream.

Preheat the oven to 190°C/375°F/Gas 5.

Roll out the pastry on a lightly floured surface to 3mm/¹/₈in thick. Using a plain cutter, stamp out 12 circles to line a 12-hole muffin tray and 12 smaller discs for lids. Line the moulds with the larger discs of pastry and fill with the apple mixture.

Brush the rim of each case with water and top with the small circles of pastry. Trim with a knife to make neat edges. Make 3 small neat holes in the top of each pie and dust with sugar.

Bake for 25 minutes until golden at the edges. Allow to cool a little, then remove from the tin, dust with a little more sugar and serve warm with sweetened mascarpone.

chocolate and pecan pie

This sticky, gooey chocolate pie is perfect served warm with vanilla ice cream. As the filling is quite rich and sweet, a whole pastry lid would be too heavy – the lattice pastry topping is much lighter, as well as looking lovely (*illustrated on preceding pages*).

serves 6

for the pastry
300g/10oz sweet shortcrust pastry (see page 15), with 30g/1oz plain flour replaced with cocoa powder

for the filling
100g/3¹/₂oz light muscovado sugar · 175ml/6fl oz golden syrup · 3 eggs, lightly beaten
2 tsp vanilla extract · 200g/7oz pecan nuts, roughly chopped · 75g/3oz dark chocolate, chopped

Preheat the oven to 180°C/350°F/Gas 4.

Grease a 23cm/9in pie dish. Roll out two-thirds of the pastry on a lightly floured surface to about 3mm/¹/₈in thick and 2.5cm/1in bigger than the dish. Place the pastry into the dish and carefully press into the sides. Trim the edges and chill whilst you make the filling.

Mix together the sugar, syrup, eggs and vanilla and whisk with a fork. Spread the pecan nuts on the bottom of the pastry shell with the chocolate. Pour the syrup mixture over the nuts and chocolate.

Roll out the remaining pastry and cut into strips to form a lattice topping over the pie. Trim the edges with a knife to neaten.

Bake for 35–40 minutes until the filling is set but gooey and oozing. The filling will be a bit wobbly but will set further on cooling. Cool completely before cutting into wedges to serve.

bakewell pie

This is an old recipe from Derbyshire and I've suggested making it using strawberry or raspberry jam. You can, however, add fresh fruit to the jam to transform it into a really superior pie.

serves 6

for the pastry
300g/10oz sweet shortcrust pastry (see page 15)

for the filling
5 tbsp strawberry or raspberry jam · 100g/3¹/₂oz raspberries · 50g/2oz butter
50g/2oz caster sugar · 1 egg, beaten · 25g/1oz plain flour · ¹/₂ level tsp baking powder
50g/2oz ground almonds · 1 tbsp milk

Preheat the oven to 180°C/350°F/Gas 4.

Roll out the pastry on a lightly floured surface to a thickness of 3mm/¹/₈in and use it to line a 20cm/8in shallow pie plate, reserving the trimmings. Prick the base and cover it with the jam and raspberries.

Place the butter and sugar in a large bowl and mix together with an electric whisk or wooden spoon until smooth, light and fluffy. Add the egg a little at a time, beating thoroughly until incorporated.

Sift together the flour and baking powder, add the ground almonds and then stir into the egg and sugar mixture, adding the milk to make the mixture soft and creamy. Spread the mixture over the jam and fruit in the pastry case and decorate the top with pastry leaves made from the reserved trimmings.

Bake for 30–35 minutes until puffed and golden. Serve warm or at room temperature.

eccles cakes

They're called cakes but technically they're pies – and we love them whatever they are. There are 101 recipes for Eccles cakes, but whether they use lard-based pastry or puff, omit allspice or include nutmeg, they are all sugar-coated, crisp pastries containing dried fruit and a heady old English spice mix. To be really good, they should have a crunchy pastry coating and a moist, dense, highly spiced filling. This version is sure to bring a smile to the lips in the depths of winter.

makes 9

for the pastry
500g/1lb ready-made puff pastry · 1 egg white, lightly whisked, to glaze 50g/2oz demerara sugar

for the filling
35g/1¼oz butter
40g/1½oz brown sugar
70g/3oz currants · 20g/¾oz mixed peel · ½ tsp ground allspice · ½ tsp ground nutmeg

Preheat the oven to 180°C/350°F/Gas 4.

Roll out the pastry on a lightly floured surface to make a large sheet about 3mm/⅛in thick. Cut out 9 discs about 12cm/5in in diameter. Allow to stand while you make the filling.

Melt the butter and sugar together in a small pan, then stir in the remaining filling ingredients. Place a large tablespoon of filling in the centre of each of the pastry circles. Brush the edges of the circle with a little egg white. Working round the circle, take a section of the pastry between your thumb and forefinger and fold it into the centre. Take the next section and fold it into the centre, overlapping the previous fold. Press down to seal it. Continue until you have gathered up all the edges and have formed a parcel. Flip the parcel over and, pressing down gently with the palm of your hand, shape it to form a perky-looking, plump oval. Slash the pastry twice on the top, brush with egg white and sprinkle with demerara sugar.

Place the cakes on to a baking tray and bake for 15–20 minutes. There is lots of sugar in the filling, so watch out that it doesn't boil out of the pastry.

mrs white's treacle pie

This recipe was given to me by my friend Jenny's mum, who has made this pie forever and was happy to share it. It's a traditional treacle tart and unbelievably simple, but also a delicious classic that we should never forget.

serves 4

for the pastry
200g/7oz sweet shortcrust pastry (see page 15)

for the filling
250g/8oz golden syrup · 75g/3oz fresh white breadcrumbs · grated zest and juice 1 lemon

Roll out the pastry on a lightly floured surface to a thickness of 3mm/¹/₈in and use to line a 20cm/8in pie tin. Trim off any overhanging pastry and chill the pastry case for 20 minutes. Reserve the pastry trimmings for the top.

Preheat the oven to 200°C/400°F/Gas 6. Place a baking tray in the oven to heat.

Place the golden syrup in a saucepan and heat through. Remove from the heat and stir in the breadcrumbs, lemon zest and lemon juice. Spread the mixture evenly into the pastry case.

Roll out the reserved trimmings and cut into 10–12 strips. Twist the strips into spirals and then lay half of them over the pie filling. Arrange the remaining strips at right angles to the first strips to form a lattice. Press the ends of the strips on to the rim of the pastry case.

Place the pie on the hot baking sheet and bake for 10 minutes. Lower the temperature of the oven to 190°C/375°F/Gas 5 and bake for a further 15 minutes. Serve warm with custard.

apple and blackberry pie

Deep fruit pies made in earthenware dishes with a single crust are great for using up seasonal fruit when it is plentiful. Pack the fruit well into the dish, piling it high with only a little liquid or it will sink and the crust will fall (a pie funnel will also help to prevent this). Apple and blackberry has got to be the best fruit pie combination ever, but feel free to use whatever is in season and plentiful *(illustrated on preceding pages)*.

serves 6

for the pastry
300g/10oz sweet shortcrust pastry (see page 15) · 2 tbsp milk, to glaze

for the filling
25g/1oz butter · 1/2 tsp ground cinnamon · 325g/11oz caster sugar
700g/11/2lb fresh blackberries · 700g/11/2lb dessert apples, peeled, cored and sliced

Preheat the oven to 200°C/400°F/Gas 6.

Heat the butter in a large saucepan, add the cinnamon, 300g/10 oz of the sugar and half the blackberries and simmer for about 10 minutes until the fruit is soft. Mash with a potato masher to make a thickish sauce.

Mix the apples and remaining blackberries together and place them in 1.5 litre/21/2 pint deep pie dish and pour over the blackberry sauce. Place a pie funnel in the centre of the filling.

Roll out the pastry on a lightly floured surface to about 3mm/1/8in and 3cm/1in larger than the pie dish. Cut off a strip and press this on to the edge of the dish. Place the pastry lid on top and press down to seal. Trim away any excess pastry, brush the top with milk to glaze and sprinkle with the remaining caster sugar.

Bake for 30 minutes until the pastry is golden and the filling bubbling. Leave to stand for 10–15 minutes before serving with cream.

apple pie with cheese pastry

Apple pie without the cheese is like a kiss without a squeeze.

This is an old Saxon proverb and they certainly knew what they were talking about. This is pure unadulterated apple pie complemented by the best-ever pastry. The ancient combination of cheese and apple makes absolute sense and, believe me, is wonderful. Use Cox's apples for flavour and because they hold their shape and Bramley's to make the delicious sauce.

serves 6

for the pastry
350g/11½oz plain flour · 150g/5oz caster sugar · 150g/5oz butter, cubed
2 egg yolks · 50g/2oz mature Cheddar cheese, finely grated

for the filling
4 large Bramley apples, peeled, cored and chopped (about 875g/1¾lb)
225g/7½oz Cox's apples, peeled, cored and chopped
150g/5oz caster sugar, plus extra for dusting · juice ½ lemon

Place the flour in a large mixing bowl, make a well in the centre and tip in the sugar. Add the butter and use your fingertips to rub it into the flour and sugar until the mixture resembles fine breadcrumbs. Stir in the egg yolks and cheese, adding a little water if the mixture seems too dry. Use your hands to form the mixture into a smooth dough. Wrap the dough in cling film and chill for 20 minutes.

Place the apples in a saucepan with the sugar, lemon juice and 2 tbsp water and cook for about 15 minutes until softened. Leave to cool.

Preheat the oven to 190°C/375°F/Gas 5. Place a sturdy baking tray in the oven to heat.

Roll out two-thirds of the pastry to 5mm/¼in thick to fit a 23cm/9in pie tin or plate. Fill with the cooled apple mixture. Roll out the remaining pastry to make the lid. Brush the edges of the pastry case with water and top with the lid, pressing down to seal. Trim with a knife to make a neat edge and crimp the edges with your fingertips, if you like. Make a hole in the top of the pastry and dust with caster sugar. Place on the baking tray and bake for 25–30 minutes until golden. Leave to stand for about 15 minutes before cutting into wedges and serving with cream.

spiced summer berry free-form pie with lemon pastry

This is a pie to make when summer berries are at their plumpest and most flavoursome and it can be adapted to whatever berries you have at hand. The pie takes no time at all – great for hot days, when you don't want to overheat the kitchen or yourself. Serve it with vanilla ice cream for an exquisite taste of summer. The fruit liqueur adds a richness and depth to the sauce created by the berries but it is completely optional. A good squeeze of fresh orange over the berries works well as an alternative,

serves 4

for the pastry
300g/10oz sweet rich shortcrust pastry (see page 16), adding grated zest 1 lemon to the mixture

for the filling
25g/1oz butter, melted · 50g/2oz light muscovado sugar, plus extra for sprinkling
600g/1¼lb mixed summer berries, such as raspberries, blueberries, strawberries
1 tbsp cornflour · pinch ground cinnamon · 3 tbsp crème de cassis or any fruit liqueur

Preheat the oven to 200°C/400°F/Gas 6.

Place the melted butter in a large bowl and toss with the muscovado sugar, mixed berries, cornflour, cinnamon and crème de cassis.

On a lightly floured surface, roll out the pastry to fit a 26cm/10¼in ceramic dish, allowing about 4cm/1½in excess pastry to hang over the edges.

Spoon the berry mixture into the pastry case and fold the excess pastry up over the fruit, overlapping as needed and leaving the centre open. Brush with milk and sprinkle with sugar.

Bake for 30 minutes until the crust is golden brown and the juices are bubbling.
Serve warm with vanilla ice cream.

strawberry and rhubarb cobbler

A cobbler is a kind of pie in an unofficial kind of way and it's such a great dessert that I felt it would be a shame not to include at least one.

The scone-like topping is spooned over the filling rather than rolled out, which makes it easy-peasy to make. It's perfect for soaking up all the juices from the filling. Tart, crisp, tasty rhubarb and smooth, sweet strawberries are naturally complementary.

serves 6

for the cobbler topping
225g/7^{1}/$_{2}$oz plain flour · pinch salt · 3 tsp baking powder · I tsp ground cinnamon
100g/3^{1}/$_{2}$oz chilled butter, cut into pieces · 175ml/6fl oz buttermilk · 3 tbsp milk

for the filling
900g/1^{3}/$_{4}$lb fresh rhubarb stalks, trimmed of any leaves and cut into 2cm/^{3}/$_{4}$in lengths
500g/1lb fresh strawberries, hulled and sliced · 150g/5oz caster sugar · I tbsp cornflour
grated zest and juice I orange · ^{1}/$_{2}$ tsp ground ginger

Preheat the oven to 200°C/400°F/Gas 6.

Place the rhubarb and strawberries, sugar, cornflour, orange zest, juice and ginger in the base of a 2 litre/3^{1}/$_{2}$ pint deep pie dish and toss well to combine.

To make the topping, place the flour in a large bowl and mix with the salt, baking powder and cinnamon. Add the butter and rub into the flour mixture with your fingertips until the mixture resembles fine breadcrumbs. Stir in the buttermilk and milk to make a thick batter mixture.

Drop tablespoons of the batter mixture on top of the fruit to cover the entire surface, creating a 'cobbled' effect, and bake for 35–40 minutes until the topping is golden and the filling bubbling.

chocolate and pistachio cream pie

This pie has a deliciously creamy chocolate custard filling which is so simple to make, and it's perfect served warm with scoops of vanilla ice cream. Bake it in a rectangular tart tin so that it's really easy to slice into bars *(illustrated on preceding pages)*.

serves 6

for the pastry
300g/10oz sweet shortcrust pastry (see page 15), adding grated zest 1 orange to the mixture
2 tbsp milk, to glaze

for the filling
2 eggs · 150g/5oz caster sugar, plus extra for sprinkling · 150ml/1/4 pint double cream
150g/5oz dark chocolate, finely chopped · 25g/1oz pistachio nuts, toasted and roughly chopped

Preheat the oven to 180°C/350°F/Gas 4.

Lightly grease a fluted 36 x 11cm/14 x 41/2in tart tin. Divide the dough into 2 portions, one slightly larger than the other. Roll the larger portion out to a rectangle big enough to line the base and sides of the tin. Cover with cling film and chill in the fridge while you make the filling. Roll out the remaining pastry to a size large enough to cover the top of the tin. Place on a baking tray, cover with cling film and also chill while you prepare the filling.

Place the eggs and sugar in a bowl and beat together. Stir in the cream, chocolate and pistachio nuts, then pour into the pastry case. Brush the rim of the pastry with milk and position the lid in place, pressing the edges to seal. Trim the edges and make a steam hole in the middle of the lid. Brush with milk to glaze and sprinkle with caster sugar.

Bake for 30–35 minutes, then leave to cool for at least 15 minutes before removing from the tin. Place on a cooling rack and leave to cool for a further 10 minutes before cutting into slices. Letting the pie stand for a few minutes allows it to set, making it easier to slice. Don't worry – it will still be warm and gooey!

raspberry cream pies

These coconut-custard-and-fresh-raspberry-filled pies are a far cry from any slapstick custard version. They're far too good for throwing – serve them warm or cold alongside some extra berries on a plate.

makes 6 pies

for the pastry
300g/10oz sweet shortcrust pastry (see page 15)

for the filling
150ml/¹/₄ pint double cream · 250ml/8fl oz carton coconut cream · 150g/5oz caster sugar
1 egg · grated zest 1 lime · 200g/7oz fresh raspberries

Roll out the pastry on a lightly floured surface to about 3mm/¹/₈in thick. Cut out 4 discs large enough to line 4 individual tart tins, 10cm/4in in diameter. From the remaining pastry, cut out wide strips to make covers for the tops.

Press the pastry into the base and sides of each tin and prick the base with a fork. Fill with a ball of scrunched-up tin foil (to weigh down the pastry during cooking). Chill for at least 20 minutes before baking to stop the pastry shrinking.

Preheat the oven to 160°C/325°F/Gas 3. Place a baking tray in the oven to heat.

Place the pies on the hot baking tray and bake for 7 minutes. Meanwhile mix together the cream, coconut cream, sugar, egg and lime zest in a large jug.

Remove the foil from the pastry cases and divide the raspberries between the pies. Pour over the cream mixture and cover with the strips of pastry – you can be as creative as you like, either making a lattice topping or arranging the strips decoratively in a random pattern. Press the strips on to the edges to seal and trim away any excess pastry.

Bake the pies for 20–25 minutes until the pastry is golden and the filling is nearly set but still creamy and wobbly. Leave to cool in the tins for about 15 minutes before removing and serve warm or cold with extra berries.

peach and apricot amaretto pie

This is a pie to make at the peak of the peach season. Amaretto has a great affinity with peaches and apricots and I have used crushed Amaretti biscuits in the filling for added texture and sprinkled finely crushed biscuits on top to provide a crunchy finish.

serves 6

for the pastry
300g/10oz sweet shortcrust pastry (see page 15) · 2 tbsp milk, to glaze

for the filling
400g/13oz fresh apricots, halved, stoned and cut into wedges
500g/1lb fresh peaches, halved, stoned and cut into wedges
150g/5oz caster sugar, plus extra for dusting · 3 tbsp Amaretto liqueur · 3 tbsp cornflour
2 tsp lemon juice · 4 Amaretti biscuits, finely crushed · 15g/¹/₂oz butter, cut into pieces

Preheat the oven to 200°C/400°F/Gas 6.

Place the apricots and peaches in a bowl with the sugar, Amaretto liqueur, cornflour, lemon juice and half the Amaretti biscuits. Mix together well and set aside while you prepare the pastry.

When your dough is ready, spoon the filling into the base of a 1.5 litre/2¹/₂ pint pie dish and dot pieces of butter on the top.

On a lightly floured surface, roll out the pastry to just larger than the pie dish, then cut off a strip to sit on the edge of the dish. Place the pastry on top and press down to seal. Trim off any excess pastry and glaze the top with a little milk. Bake for 30 minutes until the pastry is golden and the filling bubbling. While the pie is still hot, sprinkle on the remaining crushed Amaretti biscuits and caster sugar. Leave to stand for about 10–15 minutes before serving with fresh pouring cream.

lemon curd and jam pies

We all remember these pies from childhood – simple pastry cases filled with your favourite jam or creamy lemon curd (*illustrated on preceding pages*).

makes 12

for the pastry
300g/10oz sweet shortcrust pastry (see page 15)

for the filling
2 eggs, beaten · 200g/7oz caster sugar · 150g/5oz unsalted butter · grated zest and juice 2 lemons · red jam

To make the lemon curd filling, place the beaten eggs in a saucepan, add the sugar, butter, lemon zest and juice and stir over a gentle heat until the butter and sugar have melted. Continue to cook, stirring all the time, until the mixture thickens – this will take about 20 minutes. Make sure that the mixture doesn't boil during this time as the eggs will curdle. Set aside to cool.

Pour the cooled lemon curd into clean, sterilised jam jars and store in the refrigerator until required. It will keep for up to 3 weeks

Preheat the oven to 200°C/400°F/Gas 6.

To make the pies, roll out the pastry on a lightly floured surface until it is about 3mm/$^1/_8$in thick. Cut out 12 discs of 8cm/3in diameter and place them on a baking tray. Cut out a further 12 discs of the same size (you may have to reroll the pastry for this) and then use a heart- or star-shaped cutter (or whatever takes your fancy) to cut out a shape from the centre of these discs. Place these on a baking tray.

Place both trays in the oven and bake for 8–12 minutes until the pastry is pale golden. Leave to cool on the tray for a few minutes, then remove using a palette knife and place on a rack to cool completely.

Spread half the discs with the lemon curd and top with a lid with, for example, a star cut-out. Spread the other half with your favourite red jam and top with the remaining lids. Serve dusted with icing sugar.

Yorkshire curd pies

These small pies are like yummy little cheesecakes. Their distinguishing characteristic is the addition of allspice which gives them a superb flavour without being too sweet.

makes 24

for the pastry
300g/10oz sweet shortcrust pastry (see page 15)

for the filling
200g/7oz curd cheese · 2 eggs, separated · 75g/3oz caster sugar · 2 tbsp double cream
grated zest and juice 1 lemon · large pinch ground allspice · 50g/2oz raisins

Preheat the oven to 180°C/350°F/Gas 4.

Roll out the pastry on a lightly floured surface to a thickness of about 3mm/⅛in. Cut out 24 rounds using a 7.5cm/3½in plain pastry cutter and use to line shallow bun tins. Chill the pastry while you prepare the filling.

Place the curd cheese in a bowl and mix in the egg yolks, sugar, cream, lemon zest, juice and allspice, then stir in the raisins.

Beat the egg whites until stiff and fold into the cheese mixture. Spoon the filling into the pastry cases and bake for 30–35 minutes until just turning golden.

Serve warm or cold.

pumpkin pie

A pie book just wouldn't be complete without a recipe for pumpkin pie. Again, there are many variations on the ultimate recipe but the theme is always the same. Sweet firm pumpkin (in Britain butternut squash is usually the best and most readily available) combined with eggs and cream for a creamy texture, and sugar and spices for comforting flavour.

serves 6

for the pastry
300g/10oz sweet shortcrust pastry (see page 15)

for the filling
750g/1¹/2lb pumpkin, peeled and cubed weight · 2 eggs, lightly beaten
185g/6¹/2oz light muscovado sugar · 100ml/3¹/2fl oz double cream · 1 tbsp brandy
¹/2 tsp ground ginger · ¹/2 tsp ground nutmeg · 1 tsp ground cinnamon

Preheat the oven to 180°C/350°F/Gas 4. Place a heavy baking tray in the oven.

Place the pumpkin in a large saucepan and cover with water. Bring to the boil and simmer for 15–20 minutes until very tender.

Drain and return to the pan. Mash with a potato masher until you have a smooth purée or push through a large sieve into a bowl for a very smooth mixture. Allow to cool.

On a lightly floured surface, roll out the pastry to about 3mm/¹/8in thick, then use it to line a 23cm/9in pie dish. Trim off any excess and prick the base with a fork. Crumple a sheet of tin foil and place it in the pastry shell to weigh it down then place the dish on the hot baking tray. Bake for just 10 minutes to set the pastry.

Whisk the eggs and sugar together in a large bowl. Add the cooled pumpkin, cream, brandy and the spices and stir thoroughly. Pour the mixture into the pastry shell and bake for 40 minutes. Cover randomly with pastry leaves or strips and bake for a further 20 minutes or until set.

As their name suggests, these pies were originally made with minced or shredded meat. It wasn't until the eighteenth century that they began to be made with a mix of candied fruits and suet — what we know as mincemeat today.

makes 18 small pies

for the pastry
200g/7oz plain flour · 1 tsp ground cinnamon · 100g/3¹/₂oz caster sugar
50g/2oz ground almonds · 125g/4oz butter · 1 egg yolk, beaten plus beaten egg, to glaze

for the mincemeat (makes about 450g/14¹/₂oz)
100g/3¹/₂oz raisins · 100g/3¹/₂oz sultanas · 50g/2oz cut mixed peel · 100ml/3¹/₂fl oz whisky
50g/2oz walnuts, chopped · 1 tsp cinnamon · 1 tsp nutmeg · 200g/7oz demerara sugar
2 dessert apples, such as Cox's, peeled, cored and grated · 100g/3¹/₂oz shredded vegetable suet

To make the mincemeat, roughly chop the raisins and sultanas and mix with the peel, whisky, walnuts, cinnamon, nutmeg, sugar and apples. Leave to stand for 48 hours in a bowl covered with cling film in a cool place. Stir in the shredded suet and spoon the mixture into sterilised jars. Store until required.

Place the flour, cinnamon, sugar and ground almonds in a bowl. Add the butter and use your fingertips to gently rub it into the dry ingredients until it resembles breadcrumbs. Make a well in the centre and add the egg yolk and about 4 tablespoons of cold water. Mix with your fingertips or a knife until it forms a dough. Knead gently and shape into a ball. Wrap in cling film and allow to rest for 1 hour in the fridge before using.

Preheat the oven to 200°C/400°F/Gas 6.

For the pies, roll out the pastry on a lightly floured surface to a thickness of about 3mm/¹/₈in (if it starts to stick, roll it out between 2 sheets of greaseproof paper). Cut out 18 circles measuring 8cm/3¹/₂in wide and 18 measuring 7cm/3in (for lids). Use the larger circles to line the holes of an 18-hole muffin tin. Put a spoonful of mincemeat in each case. Add a little extra whisky if you like. Don't use too much filling or it will boil over and burn the pies. Dampen the edges of the pastry with a little water and top with a lid. Seal the edges, brush the tops with beaten egg and cut one or two slits in the top of each pie. Bake in the centre of the oven for 15–20 minutes until golden. Leave to cool for 10 minutes in the tin before transferring to a rack to cool. Dust the tops with icing sugar before serving.

whisky-laced mince pies

extrapie

Simple accompaniments are all you need to go with your lovingly prepared pies. Creamy mash, traditional gravy and mushy peas are the perfect complement to a rich savoury pie, while an apple pie is nothing without a generous coating of hot custard. If you've gone to great lengths to make the perfect pie, you'll want to give it that little extra something to complete the finished result.

mushy peas

Traditionally served with fish and chips, mushy peas are a great favourite of mine and lots of fellow northerners. During my pie investigations it became apparent that this humble side dish is also a favourite accompaniment to savoury pies. From football pies to gourmet pies, a spoonful of mushy peas on the side seems to be essential.

serves 4

225g/7$^{1}/_{2}$ oz dried marrowfat peas · $^{1}/_{2}$ tsp bicarbonate of soda · 25g/1oz unsalted butter
salt and freshly ground black pepper

Place the peas in a large bowl with the bicarbonate of soda, cover with water and soak overnight or for at least 4 hours.

Drain the peas and rinse them well in a sieve under cold running water. Place in a saucepan and cover with cold water. Bring to the boil and then reduce the heat to a simmer for 1–1 1/2 hours, stirring from time to time, until the peas are cooked and have collapsed to a softened mush.

If the peas appear too wet, continue to cook them over a low heat to dry off the excess moisture, but make sure you keep stirring to prevent them burning on the base of the pan.

Beat in the butter, salt and ground black pepper.

mashed potato

It is essential to serve mashed potato with meat pies that have a rich gravy, as the potatoes help to soak up all the delicious liquor. A simple mash is all you need, using a good floury potato such as King Edward or Maris Piper to give a soft creamy texture.

serves 4

1kg/2lb potatoes, peeled and quartered · good pinch salt and ground black pepper
50g/2oz butter · 150ml/1/4 pint hot milk

Place the potatoes in a colander and rinse them under cold running water.

Transfer them to a large saucepan, add a good pinch of salt and cover with water. Bring to the boil and cook for 15 minutes until tender. Try not to overcook them as they will become waterlogged and lose their flavour and texture.

Drain well and return to the pan over a low heat for a minute or two to dry out. Mash well, either by hand with a potato masher or with a potato ricer. Add the butter to the mashed potato, then the hot milk and mash well together until smooth and creamy. Check the seasoning and add a good grinding of black pepper.

gravy

A jug of rich brown gravy is perfect for serving with meat pies such as the family Meat and Potato Pie (page 40) and the individual Scotch Pies (page 112). It is, of course, easy to use an instant gravy mix but this really won't do justice to your wonderful pie with its home-made pastry and top-quality filling. This gravy is something a little special and not difficult to make at all.

makes 450ml/³/4 pint

2 tbsp vegetable oil · 500g/1lb mixture of diced onion, celery, carrot and leek
2 garlic cloves, peeled and finely chopped · 2 tsp plain flour · 150ml/¹/4 pint red wine
400ml/14fl oz chicken, beef or lamb stock · salt and freshly ground black pepper

Heat the oil in a large saucepan over a medium heat, add the vegetables and fry for about 30 minutes, stirring occasionally, until they are very dark brown in colour (this is your gravy browning). Add the garlic and cook for a further 5 minutes. Sprinkle over the flour and stir it in, then gradually stir in the red wine and cook for a couple of minutes until the gravy starts to thicken. Stir in the stock in two or three batches, add some seasoning and simmer for about 5 minutes.

Strain the gravy through a sieve, pressing out as much liquid as possible from the vegetables as this is where all the flavour is.

Return the gravy to the pan and simmer gently for 10 minutes to reduce the liquid further and to create a smooth glossy gravy. Taste and adjust the seasoning if necessary.

custard

You can't beat home-made custard served on top of a fruit-filled pie. It might not have that nostalgic bright yellow colour but it tastes infinitely superior. I am sure there are some of you who will disagree and will reach for the Bird's instant instead, but for those who want to be converted, this is for you.

makes 600ml/1 pint

1 vanilla pod, split lengthways · 600ml/1 pint full-fat milk · 4 egg yolks · 50g/2oz caster sugar
4 tsp cornflour

Place the milk and vanilla pod in a heavy-bottomed saucepan and heat gently. Remove the pan from the heat and set aside for 20 minutes to allow the flavour of the vanilla to infuse the milk – you can also give it a little whisk to release the vanilla seeds into the milk.

Place the egg yolks, sugar and cornflour in a bowl and beat together until smooth.

Remove the vanilla pod from the warm milk (wash it and keep it for reuse), then pour the milk on to the egg mixture, whisking as you go. Pour the mixture back into the saucepan and cook over a very low heat for about 8–10 minutes until the custard thickens, but don't allow it to boil.

If you are unlucky enough to curdle the custard, give the mixture a quick blast in a blender to bring it back together again.

Serve generously over your pie.

index

thankyou

There have been so many wonderful people who we have met and who have helped and inspired us along the long journey to this book and we would like to say a very heartwarming thankyou to you all – in particular the lovely Anna from Cassell Illustrated for believing in the project and letting us just get on with it! Sarah Dalkin, what can we say, you were with us all the way, and Helen Trent for letting us into her Aladdin's cave of props. And to all the wonderful people, producers and fanatics we have met and who have contributed and helped us along our pie journey: Andrew and Luke at Pokeno, Brighton – you make the best pies; Ian and Paul at Mrs King's, the only Melton Mowbray pork pie; William Rose our wonderful butcher in East Dulwich; Manzies on Tower Bridge Road, London – we will visit often; the mighty Grimsby Mariners, and Matty, for getting us through the barriers and into the world of football and pies; finally Typhoon for supplying us with the most gorgeous pie dishes (www.typhooneurope.com).

Angela's thankyous
I couldn't have made so many pies without the help and humour of the wonderful Jules – you were enthusiastic throughout, even when buried under pastry, thank you so much. Loving thanks to David Herbert for your invaluable advice, support and enthusiasm and the fine collection of pie funnels. Jenny and Silvana, you are the best friends and support I could ever wish for. Big thanks to Mr James Fisher for all your help, advice and contacts. Finally, the biggest thanks ever has got to go to Vanessa for being there throughout and for sharing the pie vision.

So who did eat all the pies?
Dis and Alison for eating so many pies and loving every one, as well as returning the dishes clean; Col and Robert you were a joy to feed and such happy pie eaters; Jonathen and Penny for being troopers and managing to eat your way through a few with gusto; Gareth and Ruth whose enthusiasm for pie eating throughout was an inspiration.

Vanessa's thankyous
Thank you to Jamie, Luke and Rosie for their patience amongst so many pies and pictures. Craig, thank you for letting me get under your feet and so allowing me to get the shots. Most of all, I would like to thank Angela – who first came to me with the words 'Ness, I've got this idea, what do you think?', little did I realise what a wonderful road it would take us both down.